So You Want to Work in a Museum?

AMERICAN ALLIANCE OF MUSEUMS

The American Alliance of Museums has been bringing museums together since 1906, helping to develop standards and best practices, gathering and sharing knowledge, and providing advocacy on issues of concern to the entire museum community. Representing more than 35,000 individual museum professionals and volunteers, institutions, and corporate partners serving the museum field, the Alliance stands for the broad scope of the museum community.

The American Alliance of Museums' mission is to champion museums and nurture excellence in partnership with its members and allies.

Books published by AAM further the Alliance's mission to make standards and best practices for the broad museum community widely available.

So You Want to Work in a Museum?

Tara Young

ROWMAN & LITTLEFIELD
Lanham • Boulder • New York • London

Published by Rowman & Littlefield
An imprint of The Rowman & Littlefield Publishing Group, Inc.
4501 Forbes Boulevard, Suite 200, Lanham, Maryland 20706
www.rowman.com

6 Tinworth Street, London SE11 5AL, United Kingdom

British Library Cataloguing in Publication Information Available

Library of Congress Cataloging-in-Publication Data

ISBN 978-1-5381-2409-3 (cloth: alk. paper)
ISBN 978-1-5381-2410-9 (electronic)

∞™ The paper used in this publication meets the minimum requirements of American
National Standard for Information Sciences—Permanence of Paper for Printed Library
Materials, ANSI/NISO Z39.48-1992.

Contents

Preface

Museums are mysterious institutions. Indeed, that's one of the reasons that people love them. When their exhibitions and programs are executed well, museums are places where visitors can make discoveries, learn new things, and wonder at objects from far off places and distant times. The best museum experiences happen when visitors leave with a new sense of their place in the world, whether that's a tiny shift in perspective or a profound aha moment.

As readers of this book have no doubt experienced, the sense of wonder can be magical for a visitor. But that mystery is decidedly *not* magical for someone thinking about a career in museums; in fact, it's frustrating. For all of their wonderful qualities, museums are not especially transparent to casual observers. Paradoxically, sometimes it seems that working in a museum is the only way one can learn if one actually *wants* to work in a museum. While some people know early on in their first museum internship, volunteer position, or part-time job whether they want to make museum work a career, others end up investing a lot of time and money, and perhaps missing out on other opportunities, because they didn't know enough about what to expect from the museum workplace. This book is designed to provide a window into museums for readers who want an overview of what actually happens behind the scenes before making big decisions about majors, graduate degrees, internships, and other steps on the career path.

My ultimate goal for *So You Want to Work in a Museum?* is to attract smart, creative, *intentional* people to the museum field so that they can enhance the best aspects of museums and problem solve about the things that need improving. For reasons I discuss throughout the book, people entering the field at this point in the development of the museum field have an opportunity to make a significant impact. Those of us who have been in the field for a long time, including periods when change has traditionally been more difficult to enact, are counting on what we call "emerging museum professionals" to lead the way.

When I say "intentional," I mean that I strongly believe that prospective museum employees should be well informed, not only so they can answer that irksome question from relatives at Thanksgiving dinner—"So, what are you going to do with that art history [or history, or anthropology, or other seemingly esoteric field] degree?"—but also so that they can go in with clear eyes and full hearts. People who enter the field with a good understanding of what museums are like behind the scenes can better take advantage of the many wonderful things museums have to offer their staff: working in a fascinating environment, surrounded by world-class art, historically significant artifacts, or sites where landmark events took place; collaborating with some of the smartest, most creative, and most dedicated people in any field; being a part of learning community within a mission-driven educational institution; attending lectures, openings, and countless other types of fun events; and, the best part, in my opinion, having a positive impact on individual visitors and the community at large. Throughout my career, I have had many moments where I've stopped during the workday to reflect on how lucky I am to not only be doing something almost unimaginably exciting—meeting one of my favorite artists, looking through objects in collection storage, seeing a visitor make a personal connection to an object or be inspired by a program—but that I'm also getting paid to do it. While that doesn't describe every day, most museum people I know have similar moments of reflection on a regular basis.

Another goal of this book is to make the museum workplace more accessible to readers by highlighting its complexity. Lest that seem like a contradiction, let me explain: when non-museum people think about working in a museum, they probably think of only a few roles: curator, conservator, director, or possibly the floor staff (front desk, tour guide) they encountered at their last museum visit. These are the most visible roles, but they make up only a fraction of the entire staff at a museum. There are scores of other jobs that are absolutely crucial to making a museum function. Because those jobs are usually behind the scenes, it may not occur to a student or recent graduate that their skills and interests might be relevant to museum work. For example, an outstanding debater might find she has an affinity for a job in museum public relations, or a skilled contractor could be the perfect candidate for a role as a museum facility manager. One of the best things about museums is that employees come to them from so many different backgrounds. I've worked alongside filmmakers, vocalists, reenactors, dancers, musicians, writers, athletes, and numerous artists, many of whom landed in museums by happy accident. Their training might seem unrelated to museum work on the surface, but all of them found synergistic connections to the field. Arguably, this variety of backgrounds makes museums more interesting, more versatile, and more resilient than if everyone followed the same path.

For each job I discuss in chapter 3 through chapter 11, I list the personal qualities that might make a person a good fit for that job, as well as the skills and experience suggested or required. I hope that readers will see some of their own best qualities and interests reflected in the detailed descriptions of each job, and use those discoveries as a jumping off point for further exploration. I recommend that readers go through *all* of the job descriptions, even the ones they think they aren't interested in. In explaining jobs that aren't often covered in the literature, I hope that readers may make unexpected connections to roles they hadn't considered before.

Each job description ends with a "keep in mind" section. This section is intended to point out aspects of the job that readers may not have thought of, but that could have a significant aspect on an employee's career and quality of life. The points in this section aren't objectively pros or cons; each person can decide whether these factors are assets or deal breakers. For example, a job that may require weekend work could be undesirable for some people, but it could be perfect for someone else. In these lists I often point out when a job is relatively easy to transfer into another field, and when it's not. All other things being equal, I encourage people to strongly consider jobs that have significant transferable skills. Hopefully readers who decide that museums are the right path for them will stay in the field for the long haul, but that's not something we can predict. Especially as employees get older, life circumstances become more complicated to coordinate. Flexibility provides options to people who need or want to pivot away from museums for personal reasons (a spouse gets a job in another city and the family decides to move) or professional ones (an employee has outgrown their job at the only museum in town). I would argue that most museum jobs have a high degree of transferability; however, given my theory that museums are opaque to most people, the question is whether a prospective new employer in another field will appreciate the transferable skills.

Another goal I have for this book is to temporarily jettison the idea of passion. Most readers will pick up this book because they have passion about a certain topic—art, history, science, or natural history, for example—and they (or their parents, career advisors, mentors, or friends) are thinking about ways to channel that passion into a career. I understand that. I've been passionate about museums since I was a kid. I got my first museum job when I was fifteen, and I single-mindedly pursued my goal of working in a museum from that point on. My college essays were about museums, and I mapped out my art history degree requirements from the first day at my university. So, why do I want readers to table their passion? Because I feel that all too often that passion blinds us from looking critically at the field and at specific jobs. People who operate on passion alone run the risk of ending up someplace they don't want to be, or settling for less (pay, benefits, hours, job title) because they believe their dedication to their jobs fills in those gaps. That might be true, for a while, but that honeymoon phase isn't sustainable. What *is* sustainable is to read, think, research, weigh the pros and cons, look at some possible scenarios, think about the part of the country where one wants to live, figure out what salary is required to pay rent and student loans, and then making an informed decision. With that foundation supporting the passion, one has a much better chance of being fulfilled by museum work than if one relies on passion alone.

I hope that readers will find their interests and skills reflected in one or more of these jobs. But that's just the first step. In chapter 15 I list numerous resources for learning more about museums. I encourage readers to peruse some of these, to regularly read blog posts, to sign up for some of the newsletters I suggest, and to investigate some of the books. By paying attention to one's interest level—which newsletters compel an immediate click through and which linger unread in the in-box—readers will start to get a sense of their affinities. Each of these resources leads to others (for example, most of the blogs have blog rolls), so, with a little investigation, finding one that speaks to particular interests should be fairly easy.

Undoubtedly, many readers already have some first-hand museum experience, not only as a visitor, but also perhaps through a course or an internship. If not, a further step to learning about museums is to seek out any opportunity to see behind the scenes. This doesn't have to entail a huge investment of time; it could simply mean striking up a conversation with a museum staff person on a visit, or volunteering to help with a one-day festival or event. As you'll read, one of the absolute best things about museums is the generosity of the people. Ask politely and well enough in advance, and most museum staffers will gladly provide insight about their jobs over coffee.

As a museum person, it's frankly hard to imagine that someone might read this book and not get excited about the prospect of a museum career. But I admit that's possible. However, for a reader to experience that reaction is a valuable outcome in itself. Whether or not a museum career is on the horizon, the information in this book can help readers better appreciate museums and what makes them tick, which in turn leads to a greater understanding of museums' roles in our communities. Anyone can be a museum ambassador, if not a staff person, by visiting museums, attending events, purchasing memberships, making financial donations of any amount, and—perhaps most importantly—talking about museums to family, friends, and colleagues. Despite all our marketing and social media campaigns, word of mouth is still one of the primary ways that people learn about museums.

Though it's beyond the scope of *So You Want to Work in a Museum?* readers should also keep in mind that there is an industry of companies and professionals who support museums. As I cover in the text, museums often work with skeleton staffs, meaning that they may not have all of the required skills in house. Instead, they rely on contract help from companies and individuals. For example, a small museum might hire an exhibition design firm to help plan and produce an exhibition. This practice extends to almost every role in a museum. Working *with* rather than *in* museums is another way to support the field. The American Alliance of Museums' Museum Marketplace (museummarketplace.com) is a good place to start to learn more about this aspect of museum work.

I am so pleased that a number of museum staff from across the country have provided insight about their jobs for the profiles included in most of the chapters. There is no better way to give a glimpse into a job than to hear from people who inhabit it day in and day out and who are willing to be honest about what they like and don't like about it. Thank you to everyone I profiled in this book for their thoughtful input.

1

From Art to Zoology

Types of Museums

A recent graduate just entering the field will undoubtedly be thrilled to land that first museum job, regardless of where the museum is or what type of objects it displays. While there are benefits to being open to many different options at the beginning of one's career, understanding the different ways that museums are categorized can help demystify the museum landscape and make it easier to begin to sketch out a career roadmap. In this chapter, we'll look at a few different ways to categorize museums, and how the differences within each category may have an impact on their employees.

Perhaps the most straightforward way to categorize museums is by type or subject matter. The extent to which staff will work directly with the subject matter depends on their specific positions. Curators, conservators, and—to a lesser extent—educators usually need to have a specialized academic background, or at least a very strong interest, in the subject area of the museum's collection. Positions that are more behind the scenes are more easily transferable among different types of museums. A development officer in a science museum, for example, doesn't need to have a science background; however, being enthusiastic and articulate about the museum's mission will help that officer appeal to donors and write compelling grant proposals.

MUSEUMS BY SUBJECT MATTER

Art museums (Fig. 1.1) collect and display works of art from across cultures, geography, and time. Many art museums are "encyclopedic," holding collections from antiquity to contemporary art, often displayed in chronological order. Others specialize according to culture, region, type or medium of art, and/or time period. Art museums may focus on the work of a single artist. Many art museums began as private collections and therefore reflect the personal—sometimes idiosyncratic—interests of the founder(s). Some art museums have a static collection, whereas others continue to collect today. Most art museums display both their permanent collection and short-term special exhibitions, either drawn from their own archives or borrowed from other museums or private collections. Art museum audiences tend to be older than audiences at other types of museums, but school groups and families are regular visitors as well.[1]

Natural history museums (Fig. 1.2) focus on the history of scientific discoveries and include collections of animal, mineral, geological, archaeological, and other types of specimens. Specialists on staff have backgrounds in science and its history. Natural history museums may also include ethnographic material and objects that have artistic as well as scientific value. This type of museum tends to be quite popular with school groups and families, so educators in these museums should be comfortable working with school-age kids. While natural history museums can be of any size, some of the largest and most-visited museums in the United States fall into this category.

Science museums or *science centers* (Fig. 1.3) have some overlap with natural history museums but tend to focus more on hands-on exhibits to teach scientific principles and the scientific process. Exhibits often cover topics that are relevant to visitors' everyday lives, like weather, ecology, human nutrition, or electricity. Science museums

Figure 1.1. Nick Cave's *Soundsuit* in the *Third Space* exhibition at the Birmingham Museum of Art
Courtesy of Birmingham Museum of Art

Figure 1.2. Glass Flowers: The Ware Collection of Blaschka Glass Models at Harvard Museum of Natural History
Copyright President and Fellows of Harvard College

Figure 1.3. A visitor at the "Theater of Electricity" at the Museum of Science, Boston
Courtesy of Museum of Science, Boston, and Matthew Modoono

often feature at least some exhibits with a local focus, for example, looking at animal habitats representative of those in the museum's area. Science museums typically have some living collections (animals, plants, insects, fish, butterfly gardens), and many have natural history collections that help illustrate scientific concepts and that likely also reflect the history of the museum and its collection. They may also have planetaria, IMAX theaters, or other types of shows or demonstrations. Like natural history museums, staff specialists have backgrounds in science or science education. Families and school groups make up a large part of the visitorship.

Children's museums (Fig. 1.4) are a relatively new category of museum; the Brooklyn Children's Museum, founded in 1899, is the oldest.[2] Many started as local grassroots organizations, and then grew and professionalized over the past several decades. Children's museums are primarily hands-on, with a focus on open-ended play for kids from birth to age ten and their caregivers. The spaces are often divided by age, with appropriate activities and environments for infants, toddlers, and grade school children and their families. Exhibits support a range of developmental stages and activities, from fine motor activities like building with construction toys to gross motor activities like climbing structures. Pretend play (grocery stores, castles) and sensory play (water tables, sandboxes) are common features. The older, more established children's museums often have small collections of objects, such as historic toys or dolls, or even natural history objects. Specialized staff in children's museums usually have backgrounds in early childhood or elementary education. Most children's museums are engaged in extensive community outreach. Of course, frontline staff need to be comfortable working with young children and their caregivers.

History museums (Fig. 1.5)—sometimes still called *historical societies*—tell the stories of a particular place (the town, city, or region where they are located), time period (a living history museum that interprets a particular era), or event (like a Civil War battle). History museums collect objects, ephemera, and documents, and may have special exhibitions as well as permanent exhibitions. Place-based history museums often collect and interpret materials from the town or city's present or

Figure 1.4.   A family enjoys "Playscape" at The Children's Museum of Indianapolis
Courtesy of The Children's Museum of Indianapolis

Figure 1.5.   The Museum of History & Industry in Seattle
Courtesy of Museum of History & Industry, Seattle

recent past, as well as from earlier periods. Living history museums evoke towns or communities from a particular era of history, usually with a variety of different structures (homes, town hall, farm buildings) that create immersive environments for visitors. This type of museum often uses costumed interpreters, primarily in third person (staff dress in historically accurate clothing but interpret the past from a contemporary viewpoint), though some use first-person interpretation (staff assume the roles of individuals who would have lived at that period) in some parts of the museum, if not throughout. These are working museums, where frontline staff perform farming chores, cook, and engage in traditional crafts (like blacksmithing) as part of the interpretation. History museums that focus on an event, like an historic battle, may also use reenactors at times, but focus on exhibitions, collections, and place-based interpretation. Collection objects are displayed throughout the museum buildings and may also be shown in a gallery setting. History museums are popular with school groups, especially at the grade level that includes curriculum connections to local history. Staff specialists are historians; depending on the museum and how staff are deployed, employees may also have an acting or theater background, or experience with farming, crafts, or domestic arts.

Historic house museums (Fig. 1.6) overlap with history museums in many ways, but also have some unique characteristics. Many history museums—especially historical societies in smaller towns—are located in historic houses or structures (churches, libraries, municipal buildings). Other types of historic house museums are those

Figure 1.6.   The Florence Griswold House in Old Lyme, CT
Courtesy of Florence Griswold Museum

where an influential person (a writer, an artist, a president) was born, lived and worked, or died. Or the house may have been preserved as a museum not because of the significance of its former occupant(s), but because it is representative of a particular architectural style. Historic house museums tend to have tiny staffs; they may be all volunteer run, or have only one or two paid staff members. Specialists in historic house museums likely have backgrounds in historic preservation, architecture, historic furnishings, or the particular history of the place or the people associated with the house. Staff at historic house museums affiliated with a particular person are (or become!) experts in that person's work and contributions to history. By their nature, historic houses were designed to be residential spaces, not museums. Therefore, staff have to think creatively about how to use the spaces to exhibit and interpret objects, and to make the space welcoming and accessible for visitors, while also maintaining the historic integrity of the house. Also, perhaps obviously, staff have to be amenable to working in an antique structure, whether that means walking up narrow staircases or hiring highly skilled contractors or restorers to carry out repairs. Visitors typically come in small groups; school groups from within the town or city where the house is located may visit as well. Jobs at historic house museums (especially small ones) may be part-time and/or seasonal.

Specialized museums (Fig. 1.7) are museums with extremely narrow subject matter. Think of a topic, and there is probably a museum devoted to it somewhere in America. For the purposes of this book, I'm referring to professionally run, non-profit museums that meet generally accepted standards of operation, not amateur museums or corporate museums (though those can be fun to visit too). There are some broad categories of specialized museums, such as maritime museums, military museums, aviation museums, or car museums; there are also hundreds of completely idiosyncratic museums, from the Kregel Windmill Factory Museum in Nebraska City, Nebraska, to the American Precision Museum in Windsor, Vermont. While museums in the larger categories mentioned may be located in larger cities (the Smithsonian has some enormous specialized museums, like the National Air & Space Museum or the National Postal Museum), extremely specialized museums are likely to be smaller, and perhaps located in smaller towns. From an employment point of view, larger specialized museums will hire staff with backgrounds and experience in the subject area they cover. Smaller, more esoteric museums may not expect to find subject specialists, but will be looking for curators and educators with related backgrounds and the aptitude to develop a specialty. These museums can be wonderful training grounds because they allow staff to develop depth in one content area. On the flip side, though, employees who plan to eventually work at another type of museum need to be aware of keeping their professional networks and interests broad, so future employers don't perceive them as having skills that are too specialized.

Museums with living collections include *botanic gardens*, *arboreta* (singular: *arboretum*, a type of botanic garden that specializes in trees), *zoos*, and *aquaria*. Like

Figure 1.7.   The Mütter Museum of Medical History is an example of a specialized museum

Courtesy of Mütter Museum of The College of Physicians of Philadelphia science museums, staff specialists in these museums are scientists or science educators in the relevant field, such as horticulture, arboriculture, biology, zoology, veterinary medicine, or marine biology. Most museums with living collections have an emphasis on environmental stewardship and sustainability as a key component of their missions. From a practical standpoint, frontline and collections staff of museums with living collections should be comfortable working outside; all staff will likely be affected by some level of seasonality: even if the institution is open year-round, hours and visitation may fluctuate substantially with the seasons. Many of the jobs discussed in this book will be relevant to museums with living collections. However, because zoos and aquaria are accredited by the Association of Zoos and Aquariums (AZA) rather than by the American Alliance of Museums (AAM), jobs unique to them will not be covered specifically.

Keep in mind that many museums transcend or combine these categories: botanic gardens might have art galleries; science museums might have natural history collections; children's museums often have exhibits featuring science concepts; specialized museums might focus on a specific type of art. Some institutions have multiple museums under one umbrella: for example, the Springfield Museums in Massachusetts are comprised of two art museums, a history museum, a science museum, a sculpture garden, and "The Amazing World of Dr. Seuss." Museums with combinations of collection types can be especially attractive places to work because of the potential to gain experience in multiple areas at the same time.

MUSEUMS BY SIZE

What do we mean when we say museums are "small," "mid-sized," or "large"? (Keep in mind that this book does not include museums with all-volunteer staffs, which are usually among the smallest museums; though these museums are not relevant to discussions of paid employment as long as they continue to rely on volunteers, they can be good places to intern or volunteer.) The first metric we'll look at is staff size. Let's expand our discussion to define five categories of size, based on data provided by AAM about accredited museums.[3]

We'll call the first category "micro," meaning museums with one to five full-time staff members. According to AAM, as of August 2018, 15 percent of accredited museums fit this category. Next is "small," or between six and thirty full-time staff. AAM puts 49 percent of accredited museums at this size.[4] "Mid-size" we'll define as thirty-one to one hundred full-time staff, representing 35 percent of accredited museums. "Large" museums have between 101 and two hundred full-time staff, accounting for 6 percent of accredited museums, and what we'll call "jumbo" museums have more than two hundred full-time staff, also representing 6 percent of accredited museums.[5]

Another way to parse museum size is by budget. Let's also break this scale into five categories, though it's important to note that the staff size and budget size categories do not necessarily correlate; that is, it's possible—though not probable—that a museum with ten staff members (small, per our definition) could have a $1.5 million budget (mid-size). Generally speaking, though, museums with fewer staff tend to have smaller budgets, and museums with more staff typically have larger budgets. We'll call budgets of less than $350,000 "micro" (8 percent of accredited museums, according to AAM), $350,000 to $999,999 "small" (24 percent), $1 million to $4.9 million "mid-size" (42 percent), $5 million to $14.9 million "large" (17 percent), and more than $15 million "jumbo" (10 percent).[6]

What do these size designations mean for prospective museum staff? There are a couple of important considerations. In general, the fewer employees there are, the broader the scope of each position will be; conversely, the more employees there are, the more narrowly defined each job will be. For example, if a museum has one employee, that person essentially acts as director, curator, educator, fundraiser, and probably also takes out the trash (a rite of passage for many museum folks!). In a museum with two hundred staff people ("jumbo"), each of the functions I've just described would have its own entire department—with multiple levels of staff—devoted to it. The implications of the relative breadth of each position goes beyond personal preference for working with small or large groups of people: small museums enable employees to see first-hand how all the different parts and functions of a museum work together, whereas large museums enable workers to specialize and to develop or enhance expertise in one area. One is not better than the other; they're just different. My personal recommendation is that all museum workers should try, at some point in their careers, to experience museums of different sizes, because they hone distinct sets of skills.

There are also social and interpersonal implications related to museum size. Working at a micro museum can be isolating; though it's exhilarating to get such diversity of experience, staff at small museums need to make an extra effort to remain engaged with colleagues at like organizations and in regional and national associations. At large or jumbo museums, staff might feel anonymous, but there are benefits too, like being surrounded by so many creative people, and being able to enjoy an ever-changing roster of exhibitions and programs.

And certainly there are financial considerations. While not an absolute rule, larger museums often offer more competitive pay than smaller museums. Museums with mid-size, large, or jumbo staff are much more likely to offer benefit packages, and to offer them at lower cost to employees. Micro or small museums struggle to offer benefits like insurance and retirement plans to employees, though small institutions can sometimes combine forces to get more competitive rates from benefits providers.

In terms of career growth, the larger the institution, the more likely that it allows staff some room to grow professionally and to get promoted within the organization. Micro and small museums may offer no next steps, requiring employees to leave their institutions in order to move up. This dovetails with another consideration: location. Though there are certainly examples of small museums in big cities and large museums in rural areas, for the most part, smaller museums tend to be more isolated and in less museum-dense areas, whereas larger museums are often in more populous and museum-dense areas. Beyond personal preference for a rural versus an urban setting, location may not matter much for one's first job, but can be a significant consideration for subsequent positions. A museum staff person who lives in a large urban area will have numerous museums to consider when the time comes to look for their next job. Conversely, if an employee lives in a small town and works at its only museum, a new job will either mean moving or enduring a long commute.

TYPE OF GOVERNANCE

We can also categorize museums by governance type, which can affect different aspects of employees' experiences from applying and onboarding to professional development and promotion opportunities. Most museums in the United States are private non-profits governed by volunteer boards of trustees.[7] As a unit, boards have legal and financial responsibility for the museum; they establish policy, define the mission, ensure legal compliance, responsibly steward the resources of the museum, and ensure long-term sustainability. Collectively, they supervise (including hiring, evaluating, and, if necessary, terminating) the executive director or chief executive officer. Boards are responsible for governance of the museum, but they delegate the day-to-day management, including supervision of all other staff, to the director. Boards operate under bylaws and current members nominate new members, who need to be approved by the full board; typically board members serve terms of about three years, which can often be renewed. Boards vary in size, often in correlation to the size of the museum, and are typically subdivided into committees that focus on particular aspects of the museum (like finance, nominating, collections, and executive—made up of the board's officers). Each board member is expected to personally donate to the museum as well as to solicit funds for the museum from others in their networks.

Private non-profits are self-governing. While they have to adhere to applicable laws and ethical standards, these museums have quite a bit of leeway in how they hire, train, and compensate employees. While such autonomy is not necessarily a drawback, private non-profits don't have the same kind of established structures as other types of museums (described in the following chapter), and therefore may be much less transparent in their practices. Depending on the particular role, a staff person may have extensive interaction with the full board or with board committees, or may not encounter the board much in the course of a typical day or week, though the board's influence has a great impact on the culture of the museum. We'll discuss this more in the chapters that cover specific jobs.

Academic museums are owned and operated by a parent educational institution, typically a college or university (though a handful of secondary schools in the United States have excellent museums). The director of an academic museum reports within the university hierarchy, often to a dean or provost, rather than to a board of trustees. While academic museums are open to the public and welcome all visitors, their primary audiences are the students and faculty on campus. Students play many roles at these museums; they might have work-study positions at the front desk or curate an exhibition as part of a class assignment. Because they reside within the framework of a larger institution, academic museums have well-defined processes for hiring, evaluating, and advancing staff, and usually offer excellent benefits well beyond what private museums are able to offer. Academic museums may be of any discipline and are considered their own specialty; it's not unusual for academic museum professionals to spend their entire careers within this subset of museums. While the structure and processes of a college or university museum can be reassuring, there can also be a lot of bureaucracy that results in slow decision making.

Public museums are owned and operated by any government entity: municipal, county, state, federal, or tribal. These museums can again be of any discipline, with history museums and historic sites the most common. Similar to academic museums, public museums offer transparent processes for hiring, salary grading, evaluation, and advancement, and, because museum staff at these museums are part of a much larger employee pool, they usually offer more benefits than private museums. Also like academic museums, public museums can be bogged down with a lot of bureaucracy. The size of the public entity will determine the relative ease with which staff can transfer internally; a municipality may only have one museum, whereas the federal government operates hundreds. Readers who are interested in federal jobs, such as in the National Park Service or the Smithsonian, will need to research the specifics of their processes.

HOW TO CHOOSE WHERE TO WORK

At the beginning of a museum career, it's best not to get locked in to any particular subject, size, type, or location of museum. As much as possible, newcomers to the field should explore all the options and try to get a feel for the differences. For example, students choosing museums for internships, part-time work, or as subjects of course assignments should strive for as wide a variety as possible. Exposure to a broad array of museums will enable a prospective employee to make an informed decision about future job opportunities. In the graduate museum studies class I teach, I require students to base their major assignment on a type of museum where they have little or no experience. While they often find this requirement frustrating at first, most students come to appreciate the fact that they've stretched themselves in new directions. An anecdote from my own career illustrates the benefit of keeping an open mind about where to work: after several years' experience working with modern and contemporary collections in art museums I decided it was time to move back to my native east coast from the Pacific Northwest. The trajectory I had planned since my undergraduate art history days took a detour when I accepted the job of director of education at a museum of arms and armor. While my move was met with skepticism from friends and colleagues, who asked whether I knew anything about armor (I didn't, but I learned), my time there made me a stronger professional, with a broader toolbox full of transferable skills, than if I had worked exclusively at art museums. Accepting that job also allowed me to realize my personal goal of moving across country. Further, it gave me a chance to fully appreciate the variety—and quirkiness—inherent in the museum field.

2

Organizational Structure

To understand how any specific role within a museum functions, we first need a basic understanding of the entire staffing structure. As we touched upon in the previous chapter, most museums in the United States are private non-profits; this is the model we'll discuss in depth here. In parallel with the size designations we outlined in chapter 1, this chapter will look at organizational structure in micro, small, midsize, large, and jumbo museums. Note that these structures will be generalizations. Specifics vary in terms of titles and terminology, how functions and positions are grouped, reporting relationships, and other factors. Within an institution, organizational structure is rarely set in stone; it can change for many reasons, including the hiring of a new director, shifts in institutional mission or programmatic priorities, or budget cuts. Think of the structures discussed in this chapter as a kind of snapshot of a typical organization at a single point in time.

Why are we looking at organizational structure before we've discussed the positions that make up the chart in more depth? In short, it's important to know how each position fits in to the bigger picture of the museum as a whole. Since much of the work done in museums requires a team approach, there are benefits to understanding where each role falls on the organizational chart and how they relate to each other. Not only does this information have the potential to make employees more effective at their jobs, but it also may help them begin to think about their career paths long term. As we touched on in the previous chapter, the relative size of the museum dictates the breadth of any particular job (jobs tend to cover a broader range of responsibilities in smaller museums, while they're narrower in larger museums); situating the positions within a comprehensive structure illustrates that relative breadth. Also, an understanding of staffing hierarchy helps to demonstrate the likelihood of promotion within a given institution; if a staff person already reports to the director, there's less room for advancement than if the department head's *boss* reports to the director. Even though that may not be an immediate worry, it never hurts to think ahead.

What all of the organizational structures outlined in this chapter have in common is the board of trustees (sometimes called the board of directors) at the top (see Fig. 2.1). As briefly mentioned in chapter 1, the board of trustees is a group of volunteers who are nominated by their peers to serve terms, typically of three years with the possibility of renewal, and a requirement to rotate off the board after some number of terms; these strictures are designed to maintain a constant flow of new ideas and resources into the governing body. An adage in non-profit circles is that prospective board members should be able to contribute "time, talent, or treasure." That is, trustees should benefit the organization in at least one tangible way.

Time can consist of devoting a significant number of hours to the museum on a regular basis; though this may seem like a low bar to cross, since board members volunteer outside of their own work schedules, they may not be able to participate as much as they would like to. Therefore, board members who are able to invest time in the museum provide a vital benefit. In addition to serving as a board and/ or committee leader, a donation of time can also consist of attendance at museum events, and introducing people in their personal and professional circles to the director by facilitating formal or informal meetings. *Talent* means that the board member avails the museum of a particular skill set, which often means providing pro bono

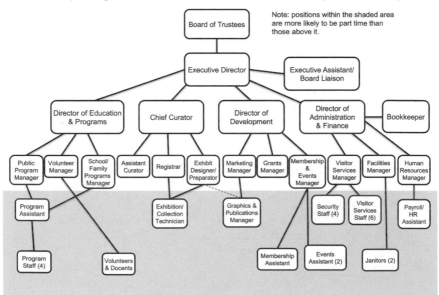

Figure 2.1.   A sample organizational chart at a mid-size museum.

professional services, such as legal counsel, marketing or human resources expertise, or financial or investing advice. (Note that the sharing of some "talents" may be limited by potential conflict of interest). Lastly, *treasure* entails supporting the museum financially, through personal donations as well solicitation of other donors or of corporate or foundation sponsorship. Ideally, all trustees would give all three of these elements to the museum, but, in reality, each individual's capacity varies. Defining these different ways of serving the board can help increase diversity: for example, a young trustee may not have the financial capacity to make a significant monetary donation to the museum, but that person may instead be able to help in a professional capacity. All board members are expected to give *some* financial support to the museum, though, because many granting agencies look at the percentage of board members who donate; this should be at 100 percent.

Collectively, the board has legal responsibility for the museum and for compliance with relevant laws, regulations, and ethics. The other major responsibility of the board is supervising the museum's director. That is, the board is the director's boss; again, this role is enacted collectively, though individual board members have different areas of expertise. It's important to emphasize that the board's function is governance, or high-level decisions and actions. For example, the board approves the annual budget, defines priorities, works with staff to craft the strategic plan, and makes policy decisions about things like human resources. The board's role does not include day-to-day management of the museum; they officially delegate that function to the director. Sometimes, especially with less experienced board members, the line between governance and management can be muddied. In that case, the director will need to work with the board to define boundaries, possibly with the help of an outside consultant who specializes in non-profit board development.

A staff member's direct relationship to the board is, like many other things in museums, determined by the institution's size. At a micro or small museum, every employee will likely know all the trustees, and the trustees will know the staff. Employees may be invited to board meetings, and each staff member probably acts as a liaison to at least one board committee. For example, a curator works closely with the collections committee of the museum, which officially accepts (or, conversely, deaccessions) objects for the collection. At a mid-size or large museum, employees below the director level will have less face-to-face contact with the trustees, though staff should know who they are. Staff may still interact with the board on the committee level, but regular interaction with the trustees will be the purview of the senior-most staff. At a jumbo museum, which will typically have a larger board (as many as thirty members), junior staff may recognize the president or chair of the board (who will work quite closely with the director), but will likely not be acquainted with most other board members.

I believe that it's good practice, regardless of museum size, for all staff members to be familiar with the board within the bounds of what is appropriate at a given institution. The higher one moves up the organizational chart at a museum, the more closely one will work with the board, so it's never too early to become aware of who they are and what they do. Depending on an individual staff person's role and the number of steps in the museum hierarchy, being familiar with the board may mean interacting with trustees on a regular basis, or it may entail simply reviewing the list of board members and their professional affiliations, which will be listed on the museum's website or in the annual report.[1] If possible, staff should try to learn who the trustees are at least by sight; this way, even if an employee is at a jumbo museum and has no other contact with the board, that staff member can at least greet a trustee appropriately if, say, they are in the elevator together.

A significant caveat, though, regardless of museum size: all substantive communication with board members should go through—or at least be approved by—the director. This means that friendly conversation with trustees at a museum event is appropriate, but unilaterally initiating communication with them about museum matters is not. The director knows all the board members well enough to know their interests, preferences, communication styles, and how their time, talent, or treasure can be most useful to the museum. At a large or jumbo museum, there is likely a staff member besides the director who is the liaison to the board, assisting the director with all board communication and business. The liaison will undoubtedly be happy to answer any questions that an employee might have about the board. The level of staff interaction with the board is partially determined by the employee culture of the museum and the management style of the director. I've worked in museums where interaction with trustees was part of my day-to-day work, and at museums where junior staffers were discouraged from communicating with board members beyond unavoidable small talk in the elevator. Whatever the scenario, staff should always be polite and positive about the museum when speaking with trustees. Complaining to a board member is unacceptable, full stop. Real problems that need board input should always go through the director.

Because we're discussing only museums with paid staff (not all-volunteer organizations), all of the staffing structures presented here also have another role in common, in addition to the board, that we've already touched upon: the executive director. (From this point on, we'll use the less cumbersome term "director.") This role can have a variety of titles, which we'll discuss in more detail in chapter 10. In a micro museum (one to five employees), the director might be the only staff person, or might be in charge of a small team. When a museum with a governance model other than private non-profit (for instance, a university museum or a state museum) has only one staff member, that person may have a title other than director, such as curator or site manager, because the organization is in fact directed by the parent organization. As a solo staff person, a director of a micro museum does a little bit of everything—planning exhibitions and events, caring for objects, greeting visitors, and offering tours—and probably relies heavily on the board and other volunteers or part-time staff for assistance. In a micro museum with more than one full-time employee, other staff will also have jobs that cover multiple responsibilities, usually ones that complement rather than overlap with the director's. For example, if the director has a background as a curator, other staff in a micro museum may focus on responsibilities such as educational programming, visitor services, or marketing and public relations. A staff of this size works as a close-knit team in an all-hands-on-deck environment, where everyone is equally likely to help install an exhibition as to pour wine at an opening. Museums of this size present an excellent opportunity to try out—or at least see first-hand—different types of roles and tasks.

Our definition of small museums spans a fairly wide range of staff sizes, with six to thirty staff. Once the staff size reaches about ten, there is likely to be separation into departments, even if a department is composed of only one or two people. For example, in a staff of ten or more people, there may be a director of education and an education coordinator who together are responsible for all education initiatives and programming at the museum. At a staff size of fifteen and up, the director often has a deputy director who oversees much of the day-to-day management; the deputy director may have a compound title, such as deputy director/chief curator. At the larger end of the "small museum" range, an executive management team composed of several of the most senior staff will work closely with the director to make key decisions.

Mid-size museums with thirty-one to one hundred staff have deeper departments. Using the education example, a mid-size museum might have a director of education, a programs manager, a volunteer coordinator, and a programs assistant, as illustrated in the organizational chart in Figure 2.1. At the larger end of the mid-size museum range, larger departments are the norm. In education, for instance, staff members may specialize by audience type: one department member may work exclusively with school groups and teachers, whereas another focuses on family audiences. With a staff of about fifty and larger, the deputy director (or multiple senior managers in parallel roles) will assume almost all of the day-to-day management, allowing the director to prioritize working with the board, fundraising, and maintaining other high-level relationships in the community or in the field.

Large museums (101 to two hundred staff) and jumbo museums (more than two hundred staff) are likely separated first into divisions, which are subdivided into departments; division heads report to the director and oversee multiple departments. For example, the director of the external affairs division might oversee development, membership, and marketing, whereas a director of administration oversees human resources, finance, and facilities. Almost all departments will have staff at multiple levels, such as directors, assistant/associate directors, managers, coordinators, and so on. While a micro or small museum allows staff to experience the breadth of a role, a large or jumbo museum allows staff to experience depth within a specialty. A caveat, though: staff in large and jumbo museums need to work harder than their small museum colleagues to avoid becoming siloed within their departments. As much as possible, they should seek out opportunities to work with other departments or at least to get to know staff in other divisions whom they wouldn't otherwise encounter. One way to do this is to take advantage of free or discounted tickets available to staff for programs, openings, and events at the museum; this is a great way to meet people, to appreciate the work of colleagues in other departments, and to develop a holistic understanding of the museum's offerings.

All sizes of museums have pros and cons as workplaces. The best way for a prospective museum employee or an emerging museum professional to understand the differences is to prioritize experiencing both small and large museums at several different points. This can be done through internships or by seeking out variety as one moves from job to job.

My first full-time museum job was at a large art museum (more than two hundred staff). The five years I spent there were crucial to my understanding of how museums work. Navigating within the divisions and departments of the museum as I worked on a variety of projects meant that I developed an awareness of the role each person played and how those roles fit together. For example, once a curator had confirmed an exhibition on the museum's calendar, she would call a cross-departmental meeting about nine months or so before its scheduled opening to introduce the exhibition, its theme, its key works, and other relevant information to about twenty colleagues from across the museum. These meetings included staff from nearly every department: exhibitions, marketing, public relations, development, education, grants, security, visitor services, the museum shop, and others. After the curator's presentation (and having received some materials in advance so as to be prepared) the other staff in the room would share their preliminary thoughts about how their department would support the exhibition. This might include, for example, the marketing manager's plans for an ad campaign, the education team's ideas for programs, development's plans for fundraising and exhibition-related events, and so on. At subsequent meetings, the staff would share their updated plans, and after the exhibition closed, everyone would debrief on the successes of the exhibition as well as on anything that could be improved for next time.

Because a large museum has bench depth, as it were, staff generally have a high level of expertise in their areas. In my first job, then, I learned skills, protocols, and procedures from people who had mastered them. As just one example, under the guidance of an expert collections manager I had the opportunity to build upon the basic art-handling skills I had learned in various internships, significantly increasing my proficiency and my understanding of best practices. Though I was only at this museum for five years in my mid-twenties, I still draw almost daily on the skills I learned there two decades ago.

Conversely, small museums gave me the opportunity to experience a variety of roles in a hands-on way, whereas I had only observed them, or been tangentially involved, at the large museum. In my first job as a department head, at a museum with about fifteen full-time staff (and about the same number of part-timers), I oversaw not only education, but also visitor services and aspects of security. The level at which I had seen these functions carried out at larger museums made it easier for me to approach my new responsibilities with confidence. To be clear, I was primarily an educator, with visitor services and security tacked on to my job description, since everyone's role had multiple facets. But though I wasn't an expert in all areas, I had intimate knowledge of how a full visitor services department worked when it had several dedicated full-time staff and a number of part-timers. Therefore, rather than being intimidated by these sudden new responsibilities, I was able to draw on the best practices I had seen in action.

My personal experience of going from a large museum to a small one made me a stronger museum professional. The opposite can also be true. Someone who starts out at a small museum and then moves to a large one brings along the first-hand knowledge of having had a more broadly defined job. Not only does that range of experience help the individual decide what aspect of museum work to focus on, but it also provides a more holistic understanding of colleagues' roles across the museum. Given the other factors determining one's career path—from content expertise to geography—it's not always possible to prioritize working at museums of different sizes. Within those confines, though, I believe that a variety of museum experiences serves an employee better than adhering to a more narrowly defined type of museum.

PROFILE

Mary Baily Wieler, Board Member/Trustee, Walters Art Museum, Baltimore, Maryland, and Park City Museum, Park City, Utah

Mary Baily Wieler
Courtesy of Mary Baily Wieler

Mary is a volunteer board member at two American museums. She has also served as the president (a paid position) of the Museum Trustee Association. Mary explains the aspects of her background that have been useful in preparing her for her museum board roles: "I have extensive experience serving other not-for-profit boards including a hospital, a library, a women's health organization, and a grant-makers' association. My career in investment banking combined with experience on other civic boards made me initially qualified for several museum board committees including finance, investment, audit, and governance."

Just as jobs in museum differ among institutions, so too do board positions. Mary says, "Board service varies from museum to museum. The Walters meets five times a year and I serve on three committees. The Park City Museum meets monthly and I chair one committee. On average, I spend twenty hours per month on my museum board work." She goes on to describe the highs and lows: "My favorite part of the job is tackling the tough issues and making decisions to ensure the financial sustainability of the museum and providing proper governance oversight of the museum director. My least favorite part of the job is chasing donors to renew their memberships."

Though prospective museum staff may think of board members only as the director's bosses, Mary encourages emerging professionals find their own opportunities to sit on a non-profit board.[2] She says, "Civic engagement is a rewarding part of one's

professional and personal life. I've made lifelong friends and enhanced my skills all in support of each museum's mission. I would highly recommend board service to anyone contemplating joining the museum field." She goes on to underscore the importance of staying up to date on legal aspects of non-profit governance: "Government regulations and [Internal Revenue Service] rulings have transformed the roles and responsibilities of board members in the last fifteen years. Board members need to be ever vigilant about these ongoing changes internationally, nationally, and in their local states."

While entry-level staff may feel quite removed from the museum board, Mary reminds us that we're all on the same team: "Museum staff members need to recognize that board members are their partners in ensuring the long-term sustainability of the museum. They are volunteers, dedicated to the museum's mission and providing wisdom and oversight for the greater good and in the public trust."

Mary echoes what most directors and museum staff would say is their one wish. Her job would be perfect if "museum board members had access to endless financial resources to ensure that the staff could implement everything they desire: all the educational programs and exhibits, acquisition of objects, and the preservation of the collections in perpetuity."

3

The Front Line

Visitor Services

Starting our discussion of specific museum roles with visitor services (VS) is appropriate: not only because these are the first staff members that visitors encounter upon entering a museum, but also because the position can be a proverbial foot in the door for all types of other museum jobs. While I don't have data other than anecdotal evidence, over the course of my career I have seen many people enter the field through VS and then move on to other jobs. That fact hints at some of the problems with museum employment—one may have to start with part-time work before a full-time position opens; we'll talk more about this later in the book. Of course, VS is its own specialty and not only a pathway to another job. As a museum division or department, VS includes the "front of house" operation of the museum, such as admissions, security, the museum shop, and the café.[1] The employees who work in these roles have a hugely important job: they set the tone for a visitor's entire experience. The difference between a helpful, friendly, and knowledgeable VS staff member and a rude, bored, or uninformed one can be the factor that determines whether visitors return. Though within the field we know that a behind-the-scenes team creates much of what the visitor sees and experiences (like exhibitions and programs), many visitors will only interact with VS staff, who serve as the face of the museum.

ADMISSIONS

Staff who work at the admissions desk welcome entering visitors and complete the transaction that is required to admit them to the museum. Usually this involves selling tickets (which may be a sticker or lapel tab rather than a ticket), though at museums that offer free admission, an admissions staffer may serve more of a greeter role. Typically, the admissions staff will process the transaction using a point-of-sale system, including applying any relevant discounts (seniors, students, members, affiliations with groups like AAA, or coupons), and will then briefly orient the visitors to what they might experience during their visit. This orientation might include handing out a map or an audio tour, recommending where to start the trip through the museum, alerting visitors to any special activities taking place that day, directing them to amenities like the restrooms, or showing them to lockers to store their oversize bags.

Admissions staff need to be well versed in what is happening in the museum, including basic knowledge of exhibitions, programs, "frequently asked questions," which exhibitions or objects are the most popular, and so forth. This knowledge should extend to the museum's neighborhood, as visitors will want information about where to eat nearby or may need driving directions when they leave. Because this position encounters all visitors entering the museum, staff must be sensitive to the needs of diverse audiences, whether that means communicating with visitors who speak a language other than English or securing a loaner wheelchair for an elderly visitor.[2]

Of paramount importance in this job is the ability to offer excellent customer service, to problem solve, and to know how to diffuse difficult situations if visitors have complaints. Admissions staff must be able to multi-task—for instance, answering a question from one visitor while processing another's credit card. They must be clear communicators, primarily in-person, but also on the phone or via email. Admissions staff must be able to stay calm and be efficient during the museum's busiest days (the day after Thanksgiving is notorious for crowds), but also stay engaged during days that can be mind-numbingly slow (say, a winter Tuesday afternoon the day after a blizzard). At some sites, admissions staff might work at an outdoor kiosk, like at the entrance to the parking lot, rather than in an office environment; at other sites, admissions jobs might be seasonal.

Though maintenance isn't a key part of this job, admission staff are responsible for the upkeep of the front desk area, as a visitor's first impression upon entering the building is so important. This includes tasks like refilling brochure racks, updating electronic displays with information about the day's events, or throwing away the coffee cups that were just politely confiscated from visitors who didn't know beverages aren't allowed in the galleries. There might be some crowd control required on very high-volume days, like those with free admission, or the last few days of a blockbuster exhibition. This could mean helping move lines along or using a mobile device to process payments away from the desk. At two of the museums I've worked at I experienced twenty-four-hour long special events: one for the last day of a record-breaking Impressionist exhibition, and the other when a new building opened. In both cases, admissions staff oversaw the block party atmosphere, with music, giveaways, and street performers entertaining visitors waiting in long lines.

At the managerial level, the head of admissions oversees all front desk staff, including hiring and training employees and creating work schedules. The admissions manager also spends a significant amount of time working with data: the number of visitors is one of the key metrics museums use to gauge success, track growth (or contraction), and determine the budget. This data can be used in countless ways across the museum. For example, a grant writer completing a grant report may need to know how many kindergarten to twelfth-grade students and teachers visited the museum between January and March of the previous year. The executive director reports admissions data to the board at every board meeting. A curator deciding when to open an exhibition may want to know the average number of visitors over the last five years in May compared to June. The museum's annual report typically includes visitor numbers for the past fiscal year. The admissions manager serves as the clearinghouse for all of this data and needs to be adept at running reports from the point-of-sale software and compiling it in whatever format will be useful to the requester.

Such data is also important for the marketing department. For example, if the marketing manager (a role we'll discuss in chapter 8) spends one thousand dollars to print a coupon for discounted museum admission in a local magazine, they will want to know whether that investment was effective: did the coupon bring in enough visitors to at least recoup, if not exceed, the cost? One way of tracking the return on investment is to include a discount code on the coupon in fine print; the admissions staff tracks the code as part of the ticket sale, therefore creating a record of its use. The admissions manager can then use that information to respond to the marketing manager's request for the number of visitors who used that coupon during a certain time frame.

A job as an admissions staff member may be a good fit for a person who:

- Finds working with people to be energizing
- Understands that the role is crucial to setting the tone for the visitor's experience
- Communicates clearly
- Loves learning about everything the museum has to offer and can convey that excitement to visitors
- Is efficient with transactions and can multi-task
- Remains unfazed by whatever the day has to offer, be it crowds or crickets
- At the manager level, is skilled at tracking and reporting data, and excels at training and supervising junior staff to provide the best customer service

Skills and experience that may help a candidate get hired in admissions:

- Customer service
- Cash handling and credit card processing, including carrying out opening and closing procedures
- Point-of-sale software experience
- Knowledge of the neighborhood around the museum
- Ability to speak more than one language is a plus
- High school diploma or GED, with a BA possibly preferred or in progress (this can be a good job for college or graduate students)

Keep in mind:

- Work schedules are not likely to be nine to five, Monday through Friday; at least one weekend day is standard.
- Holiday work may be required.
- The majority of the work takes place sitting at a desk.
- Depending on the size of the museum and the parameters of the job, these positions may be part-time, without benefits.
- Entry-level admissions jobs are hourly and usually pay minimum wage or slightly higher.
- There may be little room for advancement within admissions.

MUSEUM SHOP

Museum shops vary enormously in size, from a single rack of postcards in a micro museum to a multi-site retail operation in a jumbo museum; some museums even have satellite shop locations in another part of the city or at the airport. What makes museum shops different from other retail is that they are designed, through the income they earn, to support the mission of the museum; all net profits go back to the museum, thereby offsetting some of the costs for exhibitions, programs, and other mission-critical endeavors. Museum shops also support the mission of the museum by offering related merchandise, aimed at shoppers who are enthusiasts of the subject as well as more casual visitors who want to bring home a souvenir. Often this merchandise will feature collection images or the museum's logo on postcards, T-shirts, tote bags, and umbrellas. A section of the shop will undoubtedly be devoted to books about the topic(s) covered by the museum's collection. Many special exhibitions at mid-size and larger museums have accompanying catalogs with essays by the curators and reproductions of the objects in the exhibition.

Merchandise in museum shops may have a thematic—rather than a direct—tie in to the museum. For example, a shop in a design museum may feature all sorts of beautifully designed items from baby toys to coffeepots. A museum with a large collection of textiles may offer scarves or fabric by the yard. At the Museum of Russian Icons, where I worked for ten years, the shop sold all types of items—from lacquer boxes to nesting dolls—that were made in Russia. Depending on the museum, the primary patrons of the shop might be school-age kids buying one dollar pencils or collectors buying museum-quality art or jewelry.[3] Typically shops offer a range of merchandise types and price points to accommodate most visitors.

At entry level, the role of a museum shop staffer is similar to an admissions staffer: processing transactions, answering questions, providing information about the museum. Shop staff have responsibilities common to all retail environments—for example, pricing merchandise and restocking shelves. In a micro or very small museum, admissions staff may double as shop staff; in that case, there would be a single point of sale, and shop merchandise would be displayed at or near the front desk. Unlike admissions staff, shop staff have more of an active sales role: for example, showing merchandise from cases or letting visitors know that if they become members they will receive a shop discount.

At the managerial level, a more senior staff person will serve as the buyer, who researches, selects, and purchases merchandise via wholesale accounts. The buyer may also travel to gift shows, commission items from local artisans, and work with vendors to create logoed items. The manager also determines pricing, monitors the shop's budget (both income and expense), and designs merchandise displays.[4] The shop manager oversees the retail staff that help customers and make sales, and is typically the person who hires, trains, and schedules staff. The shop manager may also plan events (sometimes in conjunction with the education staff, depending on the specifics) such as book signings with authors, trunk sales, or special members-only holiday shopping evenings featuring discounts and refreshments.

The shop manager oversees the shop budget and is responsible for meeting sales targets on a monthly and annual basis. Indicators that the shop manager will regularly track including the profit margin, or the gross shop income relative to the cost of goods (50 percent is typically the target), and average sales per visitor. The manager also controls inventory, making sure to have enough items in stock, but also not keeping too much product on hand, especially if it's related to a time-limited special exhibition or event. Full shop inventory must be conducted at least once a year, on or as close to January 1 as possible.

Many of the skills, experience, and caveats listed for admissions staff also apply to shop staff, especially at the entry level. At the managerial level, add the following.

A job as a museum shop manager/buyer may be a good fit for a person who:

- Has extensive retail experience
- Is sales- and goal-oriented, ensuring the shop provides as much revenue as possible for the museum
- Enjoys learning about exhibitions, artists, and other museum initiatives
- Has an "eye" for interesting items (one clue: is known among family and friends for picking out perfect gifts)
- Keeps up with trends in retail, fashion, and popular culture
- Likes to travel
- Is good at negotiating, say to get the best price from a wholesale vendor
- A BA is likely required at the managerial level; a graduate degree may be preferred

Keep in mind:

- Depending on the size of the shop, the manager may be doing all of the above while also helping customers.
- With earned income as the primary objective, the shop manager may feel a bit out of sync with staff in "mission critical" roles.

- The job is cyclical, for better or for worse: part of every summer will be spent ordering merchandise for the winter holidays.
- There may be limits in how much time the shop manager can take off around the winter holidays, due to pre- and post-holiday sales and January 1 (or thereabouts) inventory.
- There may be little opportunity for advancement for a shop manager within the same institution.

A note about museum cafés and restaurants: From the visitor's point of view, a café, cafeteria, restaurant, coffee cart, or other food service at a museum is an amenity on par with the shop. However, we won't be covering food service staff in museums for one simple reason: if the food operation at a museum is large enough to require multiple staff members, it is almost always managed by an outside company. These companies pay the museum a percentage of their revenue, and in exchange the companies receive restaurant space in the museum as well as regular foot traffic. If a museum has very limited food options (say, self-service coffee), those sales are usually handled by admissions staff, or are sometimes handled on the honor system. Rarely is there a successful food service model between these two extremes, where a profitable café or restaurant is managed and staffed by the museum.

SECURITY

The first thing that comes to mind upon hearing the term "museum security" might be *Night at the Museum* or an art heist movie. But ask any museum security staff person what their first priority is, and they'll say that it's the safety of the people at the museum—visitors and staff. Of course, the collection and the building are important too, but not as important as personal safety.

Before we go on to talk about entry-level security staff, it's important to say that the specifics of this role vary enormously depending on the museum's size, collection, and locations. Some museums—especially large and jumbo museums—have uniformed security staff present in the galleries to protect the objects and to enforce rules. While uniformed guards are friendly and will answer questions, they do not engage extensively with visitors outside of these parameters. In fact, an outside company may manage this type of security force. Other museums have more of a hybrid greeter/information/security role, or even have interpreters (educators) who double as security staff, in that they're responsible for enforcing rules. Our discussion here focuses on dedicated security staff who are museum employees rather than contract workers.

Entry-level security staff work "on the floor," either stationed in one section of the museum or rotating through several on patrol. They are present in the galleries to ensure the safety of the visitors and of the collection. Guards will often enforce rules, especially ones that may be specific to that museum or may be less familiar to visitors: for example, not allowing bags larger than a certain size, or ensuring that visitors use pencils instead of pens when taking notes or sketching. Like admissions and shop staff, security guards need to be aware of the goings on at the museum to be able to answer questions and give directions. Visitors may not distinguish between types of museum staff, and may expect guards to know detailed information about the objects on view; though security staff arguably spend more time with the collections than anyone else on staff, content knowledge is not required, and potentially distracts from a guard's main responsibilities, so visitors' inquiries on these topics may need to be redirected.

Security staff also must be able to respond to emergencies of all kinds, from helping a visitor who falls ill to guiding people to the exits if there's a fire; security is also responsible for requesting additional assistance from police, emergency medical technicians, or the fire department. Some museums have higher-level security at the entrance, such as bag inspections or metal detectors. Though uncommon across most types of museums, these screening measures are likely to be in place at museums with missions and/or collections that may make them targets of violence or terrorism. In these institutions, security staff carry out the required screenings. If any type of incident occurs in the museum, security staff will be expected to fill out a report explaining what happened and how the issue was resolved.

Though most days at museums are uneventful in terms of emergencies or security problems, incidents do, of course, happen. Over the course of my career in museums, I have personally seen security staff respond to the following: a child fainting during a school tour, a prolonged power outage that led to the failure of the alarm system, a cash donation box being torn from the wall by a thief, a car crashing into a large air handler near the museum's loading dock, a threatening phone call made to the museum by a person who was offended by the content of a planned contemporary art exhibition, and a 6.8 magnitude earthquake. When compiled in a list, these incidents seem almost humorous, but in reality they were serious situations that security staff had to handle in a calm, professional fashion, ensuring the safety of everyone involved.

Senior security staff have a supervisory role, and, in mid-size and larger museums, they may spend more time behind the scenes than on the floor. For example, they may be responsible for camera monitoring, or they may be posted at the staff entrance or the loading dock where they receive shipments and deliveries and welcome people coming for meetings on days when the museum is closed. Security supervisors will work with the entire staff of the museum on drills and training; every museum should have a disaster plan (it's required for accreditation), and should practice it regularly. At the most senior level of a large or jumbo museum, the chief or director of security will likely be part of the executive team (the executive director's "cabinet," if you will) and will determine security policy for the museum. His sphere of influence continues outside of the building, as he will work with city or town officials like the fire marshal and the police department.

Of all subsets of museum staff, security guards are the most likely to be unionized. These unions, typically at jumbo museums in large urban areas (such as the Museum of Fine Arts, Boston; the Harvard Art Museums; Milwaukee Art Museums; and the American Museum of Natural History in New York) are aimed at improving pay, benefits, and working conditions for security guards.[5]

A job in museum security may be a good fit for a person who:

- Finds working with people to be energizing
- Remains unflappable in an emergency
- Is comfortable enforcing rules, even ones that aren't popular
- Has an interest in the museum's mission and enjoys the uniqueness of the museum environment[6]
- Is a clear communicator, both with the public and with colleagues (e.g., on two-way radios)
- Keeps up with best practices related to security

Skills and experience that may help a candidate get hired in museum security:

- Customer service, especially the ability to be diplomatic while enforcing rules
- Military service
- Emergency response training or experience (such as CPR/AED certification)
- Experience with specialized security equipment and systems (such as security cameras and monitors)
- Quick-thinking and self-directed
- The ability to speak more than one language is a plus
- At least a high school diploma or GED is typically required at entry level, and an associate's degree or a BA at the manager level

Keep in mind:

- An irregular schedule is likely, especially at museums that have security staff on duty around the clock.
- Security staff spend a lot of time on their feet—sometimes on very hard floors.
- Security staff stationed in public areas on low-traffic days may get bored.[7]
- Entry-level security jobs may be part-time, without benefits, and may pay minimum wage or slightly above.
- Ability for advancement may be limited: a jumbo museum may have dozens or scores of guards but only a handful of supervisors.

PROFILE

Phillip Aguet, Director of Protection Services, Field Museum of Natural History, Chicago, Illinois

Phillip Aguet
Courtesy of Phillip Aguet

Phillip describes his job at the Field: "I am in charge of the protection of all employees, visitors, and objects within the walls of the museum, as well as employees who are abroad doing research. I oversee three shifts of officers covering twenty-four hours of every day of the year." He goes on to explain further: "The job really is about people. Museums tend to attract and hire passionate and motivated people and harnessing that energy towards something like disaster preparedness can be a challenge when it is so often a foreign concept. That challenge keeps the work interesting and the days short."

Phillip's background combines several different skills and areas of expertise that have prepared him for his work at the Field, perhaps in some unexpected ways. He says, "My undergraduate degree is in political science. Although often viewed as a generalist degree, the portions focusing on organizational behavior and the interactions of different groups of humans has been invaluable. My training in law enforcement, paramedicine, and even firefighting has served to keep me grounded and connected to operational realities. My master's degree in threat and response management has helped me to keep pace with my colleagues' academic and intellectual points of view."

He notes that his work requires dedication, but that he tries to keep it from becoming all-consuming: "The job requires flexibility and the ability to remain available for emergencies without the work totally governing your life. It is a balancing act I am accustomed to from my time in the government." Phillip shares some sound advice for people entering the field:

> Train and learn as much as you can. Diversify your skills. Have multiple selling points for a prospective employer. Skills, degrees, certificates, languages, and documented experience make you stand out from the crowd. Also, polish your communication skills. Knowing how to communicate across many groups of people will absolutely make you a standout leader in any organization.

Phillip says that "there is no perfect job." He laments the limited pay, noting that "Chicago is not a cheap city to live in; museums try to be competitive but, as nonprofits, are not always in a position to do so." Still, the good outweighs the bad. He says, "What the job is and becomes is entirely up to me and the energy I put in. I love the idea that my time here is akin to national service. I am proud of my work protecting something that will remain long after I'm gone."

4

Education

Education in one form or another is essential to all museums; in fact, museums' non-profit status is based on the fact that they are educational institutions. That means that everything a museum does is designed to enrich the lives of the community, whether through an exhibition, a program, or a community event.

Within museums, the education department is at the heart of the education function. Think of the analogy of a university: by definition, it primarily functions as an educational institution. While everyone on staff is working toward this greater goal, a specialized group of staff—the faculty—actually delivers the instruction. Museum educators are similar; they deliver instruction in museums. Over the last twenty years or so, museums have shifted from a model of delivering information *to* visitors toward a model that strives to create meaning and connections *with* visitors.

There is a huge variety of roles within education departments—the job description of a museum educator at one institution might look quite different than a similar job at another institution. As we've mentioned before, educators at small museums will typically perform nearly all education functions, whereas educators at large or jumbo museums are usually responsible for one particular area. In this chapter, we'll discuss four roles: program manager, education coordinator, volunteer manager, and interpreter.

EDUCATION DEPARTMENT TERMINOLOGY

Before we do so, however, we need to review some of the terminology we'll be using that, perhaps confusingly, differs from ways we might use the same words in other contexts. In an education department, the word "program" refers to a pre-scheduled

31

event organized by department staff and featuring some type of educational content. Examples would be lectures, workshops, films (especially in a series or with a related discussion), and so on. "Events" usually refer to gatherings that are primarily social and only secondarily educational; the membership or development department typically organizes these. "Tours" for general audiences are facilitated in-gallery experiences led by a museum educator (either paid or volunteer; more on that later). These are usually free and provided on a drop-in basis rather than pre-scheduled. "School visits" (for kindergarten to twelfth-grade students and teachers), and "college visits" (students and instructor[s] as part of a course) are specialized educational programs designed for groups coming together from the same school or institution.[1] General "group visits" are for adults experiencing the museum together, usually with as much of a social purpose as an educational one; examples of this type of group include those from assisted living facilities, community centers or churches, or clubs like college alumni groups.

Groups often receive a discount or special pricing once the size has reached around ten or twelve people, and they may request and receive specialized content, such as a tour of a special exhibition or a focus on a particular part of the collection. Group visits almost always include a tour and may also include other experiences, such as a workshop or hands-on activity, or the use of a space in the museum for the group to have lunch.[2]

One way education departments in mid-size and larger institutions often subdivide is by audience. The main audience categories include families (elementary-age children when they visit with their parents/guardians or other family members), kindergarten to twelfth-grade students and teachers, and adults (when they visit without children). In very large and jumbo museums, there may be further subdivision by age group, such as preschool children, teens, and senior adults.

Another note about terminology: oftentimes staff in education departments are referred to, rather generically, as "educators." This term can refer to interpreters as well as to program managers and department directors. Because it's so broad as to be confusing for our purposes, we'll avoid the term, but be aware that it may pop up in job listings and in other contexts.

PROGRAM MANAGER

We'll start with the program manager role, which drives much of the department's activity. The program manager's main responsibility entails developing the content and format of the programs the museum offers. At some museums this happens on a quarterly schedule, a vestige of the time when most program information was delivered in print via the US mail and when hard copy printing required significant lead time. Now, as most program information is delivered online, the program schedule can be developed under a less rigid time frame, though most programs still are planned well in advance.

Many museums have a recurring schedule of programs that happen on a regular basis; these form the main structure of the program schedule. These might include monthly curator talks, a quarterly book discussion group, or a weekly preschool story time. Many museums also have an annual schedule, including members' appreciation days or programs that typically take place over school vacations or the winter holidays. Within this regular structure, the program manager brainstorms, designs, plans, confirms, and schedules specific programs. For example, an eight-week film festival may be on the calendar every fall, but the manager still needs to determine a theme and select the films.

In addition to the recurring schedule, the program manager also designs special programs. These may include programs around special exhibitions, themes, holidays, or museum milestones (such as an anniversary of its founding). This is where creativity and networking come in; the program manager works with colleagues to develop programs (e.g., maybe the conservator is interested in giving a lecture on a restored painting), reaches out to networks in the community (perhaps the choir from a local college will agree to perform at the museum), and taps into their own bank of ideas to try something new (say, pilot a new family program inspired by a model highlighted at a conference). After establishing the program schedule, the manager finalizes the details, such as fees and scheduling, and then works with the marketing department to get the information onto the museum's program calendar.

The program manager needs to balance programs taking place in the short, medium, and long term. For example, there may be last-minute details to coordinate with an artist teaching a workshop at the end of the week. Simultaneously, the calendar listings for next month's programs may require editing at the same time that tentative programs for next quarter must be confirmed. The program manager position requires the ability to be organized, plan ahead, and juggle many details at once. It's also a rewarding job because programs are one of the key ways that museums make their exhibitions and collection relevant to different types of audiences. The program manager makes that happen.

Depending on the museum, as we've alluded to previously, one or a small number of program managers will plan all programs; at very large or jumbo museums, a separate staff member may manage each segment of the audience. For example, one person might work exclusively with kindergarten to twelfth-grade students and teachers, whereas another might specialize in early childhood programs. Program managers working with specific audiences need to have expertise in that area; for instance, many managers who work exclusively with primary and secondary students and teachers have been trained as teachers themselves. Not only do program managers need to understand the characteristics of their target audiences, but they also have to understand the types of programs that will best suit that audience. For example, programs for students and teachers need to be aligned with national and state educational curricula.

Education staff in large or jumbo museums might specialize by collection. This is more likely to be the case in museum complexes that are composed of multiple individual museums under one institutional umbrella, but it is a model occasionally used by museums that are single entities as well.[3]

A job as a program manager may be a good fit for a person who:

- Loves brainstorming and coming up with creative ideas
- Collaborates effectively
- Is an expert planner: organized, detail-oriented, and able to keep track of different projects simultaneously
- Likes to network and develop relationships
- Has or is willing to develop a background in the museum's content area
- Is comfortable with public speaking
- Has experience relevant to one or more specific audiences

Skills and experience that may help a candidate get hired as a program manager:

- Project management, scheduling, short- and long-range planning
- Extensive computer skills (the ability to update websites is a plus in micro or small museums)
- Customer service
- Budgeting
- Formal or informal teaching experience
- Specific skills or experience in the types of programs offered (film, concerts, performing arts, workshops, etc.)
- At least a BA, with an MA often preferred

Keep in mind:

- Most public programs are scheduled during evening and weekend hours, requiring a flexible schedule.
- Days can be quite long, starting with an early meeting and ending with an evening program, with a full workday in between.
- Program managers have to be willing to take risks; some programs will turn out to be mediocre, and others might be excellent but—inexplicably—poorly attended. Chalk these up to learning experiences!
- Though it's improved quite a bit in the last ten years or so, education staff have traditionally had lower status within the museum hierarchy than curators and other types of positions; salaries might be correspondingly low.
- Because these positions require and use a broad range of skills, there's likely more room for advancement than there is in a department with a more traditional hierarchy.

EDUCATION COORDINATOR

The education coordinator acts as the administrator of the education department and provides logistical support for the programs planned by the manager(s). The coordinator is the initial point of contact for booking group visits and for registering for programs. The coordinator serves as the clearinghouse for all types of questions about the department's activities, requiring detailed knowledge of how group visitors use the museum, the content of programs, and how the museum supports school curricula. Some examples of the types of questions: a teacher asks about the timing of field trip activities so she can ensure that all 120 of her school's sixth graders can complete their visit within a three-hour time frame, a program registrant has questions about the supply list for an upcoming art workshop, a group visit coordinator from a senior center needs more information about building accessibility, or a board member wants to arrange a special tour for a VIP who is a prospective donor to the museum.

Oftentimes, these types of questions require the coordinator to act as a liaison between the person requesting the information and the education staff who planned or will teach it. For example, if a teacher requests a specialized tour outside of the usual offerings, the coordinator may have to check with the program manager or the interpreter (discussed later in this chapter) to determine if the teacher's needs can be met. The coordinator will then communicate the answer back to the requester.

In addition to fielding questions, the coordinator processes bookings and registrations on the phone or in person. (Online ticketing allows people to register themselves, but there may still be some back-end administrative work the coordinator needs to complete for these transactions.) Similar to the admissions staff we discussed in the last chapter, the coordinator needs to be comfortable with payment processing and with customer service. Just before the program or group visit, the coordinator may help with preparing materials or setting up. At the program, the coordinator may check in program registrants or groups and briefly orient them to the museum.

The coordinator's job requires two main skill sets: the ability to communicate clearly with all types of people, and the ability to stay organized and to keep track of a great deal of detailed information. The latter requires the use of some type of task management system so that the coordinator can ensure that nothing falls through the cracks. In terms of communication, the coordinator needs to handle routine requests as described previously, but also needs to be able to problem-solve and diffuse potentially difficult situations. In my experience, these situations can occur when a program registrant or someone booking a group visit wants an exception to a policy. Say, for example, that a program has a non-refundable deposit, but a registrant who can't attend because she is ill asks for her deposit back. The coordinator must be comfortable having these conversations and should know when exceptions to policies can be made or when an issue needs to go to a more senior staff person.

A job as an education coordinator may be a good fit for a person who:

- Is a people person who believes in excellent customer service
- Communicates well in person, by phone, and by email[4]
- Can keep track of many small details
- Meets deadlines and complete tasks in a timely manner
- Is interested in learning enough about museum programs to answer questions about them

Skills and experience that may help a candidate get hired as an education coordinator:

- Computer skills
- Organization skills
- Customer service experience
- Prior administrative experience
- Ability to manage time and to work independently
- A BA will be more competitive, but some positions may accept a high school diploma/GED or an associate degree

Keep in mind:

- Assistance with programs requires night and weekend availability.
- Occasionally dealing with disgruntled customers is an unfortunate part of this job.
- The work can get repetitive.
- The pay might be hourly and is probably just above minimum wage.
- Depending on the size of the department, the education coordinator may have multiple supervisors, requiring an ability to prioritize tasks and meet multiple deadlines.
- The skills developed in this position are easily transferable outside of the museum field, which could allow for career flexibility down the road.

VOLUNTEER COORDINATOR

In mid-size and larger museums, one education department member is often dedicated to working with the museum's volunteers. (In micro and small museums, the volunteer coordinator tasks probably constitute part of another education staffer's job.) The volunteer coordinator recruits, interviews, selects, trains, and supervises museum volunteers. Depending on the museum, there could be a handful of volunteers or there could be hundreds. Volunteer job descriptions vary quite a bit, ranging from casual volunteers who help out occasionally to highly trained volunteers who give hundreds of hours to the museum (often this is the case with docents, or volunteer tour guides).

One aspect of the volunteer coordinator's role is to work with other staff to determine what volunteer positions they need to have filled; what type of background, experience, and skills they're hoping to find in a candidate; and the specifics of the role (in terms of hours, days of the week, and so forth). The coordinator will then try to match colleagues' needs to the skills and availability of prospective volunteers. It's important to have a good understanding of the needs before recruiting volunteers, because the coordinator must find the right number of volunteers: too many, and they may lose interest without enough to do; too few, and they will probably be spread too thin.

Once the volunteer coordinator understands the museum's needs, the next step is to advertise the museum's call for volunteers through various means, such as the museum website, the local newspaper, or information sessions held at the museum. In some cases, volunteers are recruited on an ongoing basis; in other cases, there is a regular cycle for bringing on new volunteers (perhaps once a year, or whenever a critical mass of tasks has accumulated). Best practices dictate that there should be some type of a formal application process, and that every candidate should be interviewed. The volunteer coordinator typically conducts the interviews, and may also invite the colleague(s) who will directly supervise the volunteer(s) to join. Depending on the role, the coordinator might need to check professional references. States typically require background checks for volunteers who work with children, and some museums run background checks for every volunteer as a policy, regardless of the specific role.

The volunteer coordinator oversees the training of new volunteers and usually conducts the orientation and museum-wide training, whereas more specific training occurs at the department level with the staff who will be overseeing the volunteers. After initially orienting the volunteers, the coordinator manages the ongoing training, as well as scheduling, evaluation, and in general ensuring that the relationship is mutually beneficial: the volunteers find their posts to be rewarding and the museum finds that the volunteers fill a need and appropriately complete the tasks that they were brought on to do.

Although volunteers do not get paid, they still require much of the same oversight that paid staff would. In fact, *because* volunteers are not paid, managing them tends to be very hands-on. They need to feel that the museum values their work and respects their time by using it effectively. The volunteer coordinator often gets to know the volunteers quite well; depending on the size of the group and how involved each individual is, the coordinator will undoubtedly develop relationships with each of them, often on a personal level. For example, the volunteer coordinator will likely know which types of tasks each individual prefers and which days of the week he is available. The volunteer coordinator will be the first point of contact if volunteers need to miss shifts because of travel or if they require a more extended leave of absence because of a medical issue.

Usually, developing these types of relationships is enjoyable and is truly a win-win situation for both the museum and the volunteers. Occasionally, however, problems develop, and the volunteer coordinator must be prepared to handle them. Because volunteers aren't paid, the museum is likely not their first priority, even if they are quite dedicated to their work; indeed, one of the advantages of volunteering over part-time work is the flexibility. For example, volunteers could decide to take a month-long vacation on short notice, whereas employees would have to save up their vacation and plan well in advance for extended time off. This flexibility can sometimes leave the coordinator with gaps in the schedule or needing to find a substitute for a task. With a large volunteer pool, this is usually doable, but it can be tricky with a smaller group.

Perhaps the hardest part of the volunteer coordinator's job is when she needs to dismiss a volunteer. Though rare, this does happen, for a variety of reasons: the volunteer is not honoring their commitment to the museum (repeatedly missing shifts or being late) or the volunteer has behaved in some way that violates museum policy (say, shared confidential information or been rude to a visitor). Again, these are rare situations. More often, the coordinator needs to work with the volunteer to problem-solve. For example, the volunteer may be better suited for a different position within the museum, she might need additional training, or a gentle but clear conversation needs to take place about performance. Sometimes conversations must take place with elderly volunteers who are no longer able to carry out their duties; for particularly difficult conversations, the coordinator should get her supervisor involved, and possibly even the volunteer's family.

There are legal and ethical considerations that the volunteer coordinator needs to be aware of, even though the people she supervises are not paid. For example, coordinators should receive training from human resources professionals about non-discrimination policies and about making accommodations for volunteers with disabilities. Also, volunteer tasks must be clearly defined and may not overlap significantly with (or replace) paid staff. Micro, small, and even mid-size museums typically don't have professional human resources staff, so coordinators will need to be proactive about seeking this type of training from outside the museum. Possible sources include one of the regional American Alliance of Museums affiliates or the local Chamber of Commerce.

One of the best parts of the volunteer coordinator job is celebrating the volunteers. Often this happens during National Volunteer Week in April, but there may also be special events around the holidays or on a quarterly or monthly basis. Recognition doesn't have to be elaborate or expensive, but it's crucial to a successful volunteer program.

A job as a volunteer coordinator may be a good fit for a person who:

- Is energized by working with people
- Can keep track of multiple tasks and many details
- Solves problems without taking them personally
- Feels comfortable having potentially difficult conversations

- Effectively motivates people and acknowledges their successes
- Understands enough about the museum's mission and operations (or is willing to learn) to be able to match volunteers with appropriate tasks.

Skills and experience that may help a candidate get hired as a volunteer coordinator:

- Any kind of supervisory experience or human resources training
- Customer service
- Organizational and time-management skills
- Experience with scheduling/calendar management
- Event planning
- Volunteer experience (this helps the coordinator really understand what a volunteer needs, from training to recognition)
- Ability to be calm under pressure
- At least a BA

Keep in mind:

- Night/weekend work might be required for information sessions, training, or other tasks.
- There can be stressful moments, say, if a volunteer cancels at the last minute for an event or a crucial task.
- Because volunteers are giving their time, they understandably expect their work at the museum to be pleasurable; it can be difficult to motivate them to comply with tasks or requirements they don't enjoy.
- The volunteer coordinator may need to actively seek out training on human resources, especially at micro and small museums without a dedicated human resources department.

INTERPRETER

For our purposes, we'll define interpreters as paid staff who facilitate educational experiences with visitors.[5] They may also be called tour guides, museum teachers, docents, or any number of other terms.[6] Traditionally, interpreters served as content experts who shared information with visitors, often in a lecture-based style. Now, interpreters are more likely to act as facilitators who help visitors to make their own meaning and find their own ways to engage with the museum's objects and exhibitions. Though there is some commonality between the old model and the new model, they are fundamentally different: the older model featured mostly one-way conversation, with the interpreter as the authority; current best practice relies on dialogue, with the visitor and interpreter sharing authority.

In some museums, interpreters work primarily with school and adult groups. In other institutions, they are stationed in one part of the museum or site, and interact with casual visitors individually or in family groups. Interpreters need to be well versed in the content of the museum, and, equally important, they need to be skilled at engaging visitors around that content, through discussions, questions, demonstrations, and other methods.

Interpreters need to be wholly visitor-focused, constantly aware of visitors' reactions and needs, and able to adjust to meet those needs. For example, an interpreter who works outside at an historic site on a hot day may need to find a shady spot for visitors to gather so that they're able to focus on the conversation.[7] Interpreters must be able to work with all types of visitors, from young children to seniors, though at some large or jumbo museums, interpreters may specialize in one particular audience. The interpreter's role is essential because it lies at the heart of what museums do: foster visitor engagement. As any museum visitor can attest, the encounter with an interpreter can make or break the experience. A visit can be ruined by an interpreter who talks *at*, rather than *with*, visitors; who isn't aware of the audience's needs; or who takes offense when visitors prefer to explore on their own. Conversely, the experience can be significantly enhanced by an interpreter who points out something the visitor hadn't noticed, who asks a provocative question, or who piques the visitor's interest by demonstrating how a work of art was made or how a tool was used during a particular period of history. Interpreters need to be flexible, able to follow their audience's interests, respond to questions, or discuss an object that wasn't planned for the tour but that a visitor wants to know about.

In some museums, interpreters lead other types of programs in addition to discussion-based tours. For example, a museum may offer a workshop as part of a school visit. Interpreters who work with a group for this type of encounter may lead the workshop as well as the in-gallery discussion. Some museums, primarily living history museums, use consumed interpreters who wear the types of clothing that would have been worn during the time period represented. Other museums use reenactors or first-person interpreters (that is, interpreters who role play characters from the time period) for some or all of their visitor engagement.[8]

Depending on the institution, interpreters may use outlines, scripts, or lesson plans written by the program manager or another education staff person. Interpreters may also be involved in developing programs, especially if they have specialized content background and/or experience in working with a particular audience.

A job as an interpreter may be a good fit for a person who:

- Loves discussing art, history, science, or other topics related to the museum's mission
- Is energized by working with people
- Remains flexible and is able to work with all types of audiences
- Is a lifelong learner who believes in learning along with the visitor
- Thinks on their feet and problem-solves

- Has or is willing to develop expertise on relevant topic(s), but also understands *how* and *when* to deploy knowledge
- Understands the importance of putting the visitor first

Skills and experience that may help a candidate get hired as an interpreter:

- Formal or informal teaching experience
- Public speaking
- Acting/performance experience
- Customer service
- Demonstrated flexibility
- Experience interacting with people from diverse backgrounds in terms of age, culture, nationality, socio-economic status, and ability
- Ability to guide an interaction without dominating it
- Background in the content area of the museum[9]
- Ability to speak more than one language is a plus
- Interpreters tend to range quite a bit in age—from twenty-somethings to retirees—and so have a wide variety of educational backgrounds, ranging from high school diplomas/GEDs to advanced degrees

Keep in mind:

- Positions can be seasonal, depending on the museum.
- Outdoor museums require work in all types of weather.
- Interpreters spend most of the day on their feet.
- Schedules are often irregular and usually require at least one weekend day.
- Living history museums may require period clothing and performance of household or farm chores.
- Interpreter positions are often part-time, non-benefited, hourly positions, at minimum wage or just above.
- Interpreters may need to hold jobs at multiple museums, or supplemental jobs outside of the field, to make a livable income.
- While there may be some room for advancement, there is likely a lot of competition because of the high ratio of entry-level to management positions.

At the senior-most level within the education department, the director of education is a member of the executive team, working closely with the executive director and other department heads. In particular, the director of education is involved in selecting traveling and temporary exhibitions and advising on the types of programs that might complement them. The education director supervises all managers in the department and probably spends a good deal of time outside of the museum, working with others in the city's or area's cultural sector. In particular, the education director often liaises with school administrators and the leadership of colleges and universities. The education director likely has an advanced degree, at least ten years' experience, and possibly teaching experience as well.

PROFILE

Emily Conner
Courtesy of Emily Conner

Emily Conner, Education Associate, American Visionary Art Museum (AVAM), Baltimore, Maryland

Emily's job combines elements of the program manager and interpreter positions described in this chapter, but, as with almost all museum jobs, the specifics are unique to her position. She says, "As the education associate at the AVAM, I develop and lead exhibition-aligned K-12 school group workshops. I also write the curriculum for and manage all aspects of our education outreach program, 'Vision Explorers.'"

Like many educators, Emily's background includes teaching as well as museum-specific training. She explains,

I interned at the AVAM before I went away to The Cooperstown Graduate Program to earn my MA in museum studies. The internship prepared me to work in the museum later on—I was already familiar with the education model, the collection and the style of the department. My degree certainly prepared me to work in a museum, but my undergraduate degree in K-12 art education, as well as two years teaching in an elementary school, got me well practiced in curriculum development and comfortable in front of students. That time spent teaching also helps me relate to classroom teachers who bring their students to our museum on school field trips.

Emily's job involves a lot of creativity across different functions within the museum:

My favorite part of my job is interacting with students one-on-one and sharing the magic of our collection with them, hearing their thoughts about our artworks, and seeing the unique creations they come up with in our hands-on workshops. I also really like collaborating with other departments to pull off large events, like our annual gala or Kinetic Sculpture Race. We are a small staff, and it feels very fulfilling to work together to make a big event or public program a success.

Unfortunately, her position has limited hours that restrict what she can accomplish. She says,

My least favorite part of my job is that it is not full-time. I'd love to spend five days here working towards our goals, but I'm only here three days a week, which limits what our department can accomplish and I have to hold down another part time job unrelated to the museum field.

Emily's best advice for prospective museum staff: "Be a generalist—that is, at least have a basic understanding of what all the departments in your workplace do, and how they relate to one another. Some departments may want to work in isolation, but the truth is that we're all working to uphold the same mission, and we need to support each other in doing so."

5

Working with Objects

In this chapter, we'll look at the staff whose primary responsibilities include working with and caring for objects. The term "objects" refers to art and artifacts; when the museum owns these objects, we use the term "collection" (or "collections" if there are discrete subsets of the larger collection). Curators and registrars at most museums also work extensively with incoming and outgoing loans. Incoming loans are objects owned by other museums, individuals, or entities (such as a corporation) that the curator's home museum borrows for a period of time, usually for a special exhibition. Outgoing loans are objects that the museum agrees to lend to another museum for a period of time. At non-collecting museums, most of which are contemporary art museums, the staff works exclusively with loans or with works created by artists for particular projects.

Keep in mind throughout this chapter that museums almost always have many times more objects than are on view. The majority of the collection typically stays in storage, with objects rotated into the galleries as necessary for exhibitions and installations. Museums simply don't have the gallery space, or the resources (such as staff time and funding), to display their full collections. In jumbo museums, as little as 5 percent or less of the collection might be on view at any one time. The positions we cover in this chapter work with the entire collection, which is many orders of magnitude larger than what most visitors see.[1]

CURATOR

Of all museum staff titles, "curator" is probably the most familiar to members of the general public: curators are often the people that the media want to interview about an upcoming exhibition or a new acquisition for the museum, and they even appear in films where museums figure into the plot.[2] The curator's job is a complex one, with public aspects as well as some that take place behind the scenes.

Before we get into the details of what a curator's job entails, let's talk a bit about the different "ranks," if you will, of the job. In many ways, the curator's job is rooted in academia, and the terminology in the curatorial division of the museum parallels the terminology at a college or university. An entry-level curator is typically called an assistant curator; the next level is associate curator, and then full curator.[3] A museum with multiple curators will also have a chief or head curator, similar to a department head or chair at a university. A micro or small museum will probably only have one curator, or a director who also serves as curator. Mid-size and larger museums usually have multiple curatorial departments, always dictated by the types of collections the museum owns: the larger and more diverse the collection, the more curators—with distinct specialties—are required to work with it. In very large and jumbo museums there may be quite a few curatorial departments. For example, the Metropolitan Museum of Art in New York has seventeen curatorial departments; again, not just seventeen curators but seventeen entire departments, most of which, depending on the size, also have junior curators as well as support staff.[4]

Curatorial departments subdivide the collection in different ways, depending on the particulars of the objects and the museum. A few of the typical ways to define a curator's purview in art museums are by geography, such as the art of Asia or European art; by era, such as ancient or contemporary art; by the people(s) who made it, such as Native American art, Indigenous art, or regional art; and by medium, such as prints and drawings or photography. In science-based museums, curatorial departments correlate with the branches of science represented in the collection, such as paleontology; in the case of living collections, curators specialize in different types of animals (for example, birds or primates). History museum curatorial departments may similarly be organized by object type; this category of museum may have archivists (discussed later in this chapter) rather than curators. Occasionally, curators might be assigned to specialized collections: for example, a donor might give a large group of related objects, effectively creating a separate department; or, two institutions that merge may both want to maintain the separate identity of their collections.[5]

Curators select and display objects from the collection (or borrow them from other museums) to tell stories—about the person(s) who made them, the time or place they were made, or another theme the curator has deemed to be of interest. Sometimes a single object brings a story to life; other times the juxtaposition of objects supports the narrative. While this is the most public aspect of the curator's role—the one that visitors see in the galleries—many other types of tasks must take place behind the scenes before curators can shape their stories.

A curator's main responsibilities entail researching and writing about the collection, shaping the collection through acquisitions and deaccessions, and deciding how objects are displayed in the museum. Research may not be the first thing that comes to mind when we think about a curator's work, but it is a crucial part of what the role entails. Curators usually have advanced degrees (MAs or PhDs), and therefore they enter the museum with knowledge about the topic they specialize in, such as twentieth-century European painting. Because each museum collection is idiosyncratic, curators must get to know the particular collection with which they're working. This is an ongoing process; each object has a database record that curators continually supplement with new information as they research and work with the collection.

Much of the curators' research is disseminated through writing. For example, they write the object labels and text panels that are installed in the galleries to inform visitors about the individual objects and the thematic organization of the space. Curators also write texts for museum newsletters, websites, and journals. One important area of study at many art museums is provenance research: determining the previous owner(s) of an object, if that information is not clear. This is particularly important for objects that may have been illegally taken from their owners in the World War II era and later sold or donated to museums.

In addition to working with objects already in the museum collection, curators also consider objects that might enter the collection. If the museum has an acquisition budget, the curator may use these funds to purchase objects. For many museums, acquisition funds are limited, if they exist at all, so the majority of objects enter the collection through donations. While some donations are unsolicited, many are the result of the curator's cultivation of a relationship with a collector and prospective donor. Whether an object is purchased or donated, the curator needs to determine whether it is suited for the collection; typically curators have at least a mental list—if not a written one—of the gaps in the collection, and the priority order in which those gaps should be filled. While many generous donors offer high-quality objects to museums, curators also have to respond to—and politely decline—numerous objects that are not appropriate for the museum for any number of reasons: they might be in poor condition, duplicates of materials already in the collection, or simply outside of the parameters of the collection.

While the curator proposes objects to be added to the collection, the decision about whether to accession objects, or officially accept them, typically falls to a collections committee, which is a subset of the board of trustees. The curator presents objects to the collections committee, making a case for why the object represents an appropriate use of the museum's resources (space, staff time, recordkeeping, and—in the case of purchases—funds). At times, the curator will also identify objects that are part of the collection but which are not appropriate to keep, for one of several reasons: the object is in poor condition and unable to be treated; a better example of the same type of object has come into the collection to replace it; the museum's mission has changed substantially and this object no longer fits in the collection; or even, occasionally, the object needs to be returned to the rightful owner, as might be the case with objects whose provenance has been disputed. Objects that are removed from the collection are *deaccessioned*, a decision that also must be approved by the collections committee. When objects are sold, American Alliance of Museums best practices and code of ethics dictates that funds from the sale must be restricted to other acquisitions or to direct care of collections.

In addition to research, writing, and acquisitions (or deaccessions), curators spend much of their time working on exhibitions. Curating an exhibition involves determining a topic or theme, selecting objects that help illuminate that topic, and conducting the research and writing that will create the narrative of the exhibition. The curator also works closely with the exhibition designer (discussed in the next chapter) to determine what the exhibition will look like: how the space will be laid out, how the objects will be displayed, and how paint colors and graphics will be used to create the desired atmosphere. The curator works with educators to plan any educational components that might be added to the gallery space, such as a hands-on activity or reading area. A similar process takes place whether the exhibition is a temporary exhibition that will last a few months or a semi-permanent or permanent exhibition that will stay in place for a long time.

During the installation of an exhibition, the curator again works closely with the exhibition designer to bring the exhibition concept to life. As carefully as it has been planned on paper or on a computer screen, the real magic of an exhibition occurs when all the objects are brought together in an empty gallery in preparation for in-stallation. In my experience, the curator's sense for individual objects and how they relate to each other (sometimes described as the curator's "eye") comes into play at this point, when the objects are together in the physical space. Once an exhibition opens, the curator often gives tours, lectures, or participates in other public programs that serve as a forum to share the exhibition with visitors. In the case of a temporary exhibition, these types of programs often happen around the exhibition opening, but they can take place at any time.

An assistant or associate curator helps the curator with the tasks already described. Depending on the size of the museum and the number of projects, assistant and associate curators may have their own small exhibitions or research projects they're working on, and they'll also assist with the curator's projects. The assistant or associate curator role tends to be more behind the scenes and less public than the curator's role, but that again depends on the particulars of the situation.

A job as a curator may be a good fit for a person who:

- Has expertise in a particular area of the museum's collection
- Is a skilled researcher
- Writes well
- Has experience working with objects
- Is adept at public speaking
- Feels comfortable being in the public eye
- Enjoys traveling

Skills and experience that may help a candidate get hired as a curator:

- Academic research skills
- Ability to read (if not write) at least one language other than English (which one[s] will depend on the collection)
- Art handling experience
- Administrative/management experience
- A good visual sense, also known as the curatorial "eye" (note: this can be honed outside of the museum, too; think: interior or graphic design, art- or craft-making, antique collecting)
- Fundraising or donor relations experience
- At the senior level, a master's is usually required; a PhD may be required at some museums, especially at academic museums. At the assistant curator level, a BA is required with a master's usually preferred.

Keep in mind:

- Curatorial jobs are quite competitive. Candidates should be prepared to do several internships and to work up from the assistant level.
- Maintaining work/life balance can be tricky: the wide range of responsibilities and the pace of the curator's job may mean that quiet, focused time for writing needs to take place after hours (at night and on the weekends).
- As curators progress through the ranks, more of their time will be devoted to administration and management, especially in large and jumbo museums. Prospective curators should seek our management training and support, as it's usually not explicitly offered.
- Curators are expected to develop relationships with collectors, donors, dealers, and (depending on the museum) artists. While cocktail parties, openings, and other events can be enjoyable, they are usually after hours and can be frequent—monthly or even weekly.

REGISTRAR

Registrars at universities are responsible for recordkeeping: they keep track of course enrollment, student status, and fulfillment of graduation requirements; they process requests for transcripts and for proof that a student has received a degree. Every student interacts with the university registrar at one point or another during their college career.

Museum registrars have similar types of responsibilities, not around students and courses, but around collections and exhibitions. Registrars ensure that documentation of a museum's collection is accurate; because the status of objects changes frequently, this task is ongoing. Some of the types of information a registrar tracks about any given object includes basic data (maker, date, dimensions, materials); images; how and when the object entered the collection (donation or purchase); provenance; credit information (e.g., "Gift of Mr. John Smith"); exhibition and loan history; insurance valuation; location; condition and past conservation treatment (if any); and any other documentation that may be available, such as label copy or scans of publications that include the object.

Registrars spend much of their time working with the museum's collection management database. This database holds all of the records for each object in the collection and on loan, if applicable, including images. (Sometimes a public version of the database can be viewed through the museum's website.) Registrars need to be—or become—expert-level users of the database software. In addition to entering and updating information, they have to be able to run reports; for example, the development office may request a list of last year's acquisitions for the annual report. The standard numbering system for collections is based on an accession number composed of the year the object entered the collection, the order in which it entered the collection, and its component parts, if any. For example, an object numbered 1998.22 was the twenty-second object to enter the collection in 1998. If the object had two parts—say, a porcelain sugar bowl and creamer set—the numbers would be 1998.22.1 and 1998.22.2. When objects enter the collection, the registrar assigns these numbers per this convention. These numbers are often printed on the label posted near the object for easy reference.

In addition to working with the database, registrars do quite a bit of hands-on work with objects. For example, most museums have a regular schedule of conducting a collection inventory, in which every object is physically examined to make sure its database information is correct and that its condition is stable. (In very large collections, only a section will be inventoried at any one time, rotating every year until the entire collection inventory is complete.)

Registrars are responsible for the transportation of objects, which might take place upon a purchase, for an outgoing loan, or when an object is sent to a conservator. While professional art and artifact shippers usually transport the object, the registrar works with them to pack it (usually in custom-built crates) and to complete the paperwork required for transport. In the case of international shipments, the customs paperwork can be substantial. A little known perk of the registrar's job is the possibility of serving as a courier—essentially an escort—for outgoing loans that are particularly valuable or fragile. As a courier, the registrar will travel with the object and oversee its unpacking and installation at the exhibiting museum. While some courier trips are more desirable than others (a flight to Paris versus a three-day ride-along in an eighteen-wheeler), they're always adventures.

Registrars work closely with curators, exhibition designers, collections managers, and preparators to facilitate the installation of objects in galleries and in exhibitions. In the case of loans, registrars often assist curators in requesting the loan from the lending institution, which typically requires a formal letter explaining the reason for the request, along with a facility report—an industry-standard document that details the borrowing institution's environment (e.g., information about the climate control, fire suppression system, and security). The registrar will then track the loan requests and arrange shipment for the objects that have been approved.

The registrar also works to fill in gaps in the information about the collection. In almost any collection—especially those that have been around for a long time and were first documented with paper records—there are mysteries to be found, like objects with no provenance, missing objects, or objects that don't quite fit into any of the collecting areas and thus might be candidates for deaccessioning. Time permitting, the registrar researches these objects in an attempt to solve their mysteries.

A micro or small museum is unlikely to have a dedicated registrar; it's more typical that a curator or administrator would also handle registrarial duties. A very large or jumbo museum, conversely, will have multiple registrars, often assigned to different subsets of the permanent collection or specializing in temporary exhibitions. Note that larger museums are likely to have a registrarial hierarchy that reflects the curatorial one, with assistant and associate roles as well as full registrars.

A job as a registrar may be a good fit for a person who:

- Keeps meticulous records
- Feels very comfortable using a database
- Is extremely detail-oriented
- Has experience in working with objects
- Follows procedures: is good at executing the steps required to get something done
- Can manage multiple projects at once
- Is interested in the possibility of traveling as a courier

Skills and experience that may help a candidate get hired as a registrar:

- Use of collections databases (some job listings will specify a particular one, but the skills are largely transferable from one to the next)
- Any experience in an environment where detailed recordkeeping is essential
- Object handling
- Packing, shipping, or customs experience
- Depending on the collection the registrar works with, foreign language skills may be a plus
- A BA; an MA or museum studies certificate may be preferred

Keep in mind:

- As museum jobs go, registrars are among the most likely to have a regular nine to five, Monday to Friday schedule; there is little night or weekend work.

- While all museum staff work on teams for some projects, registrars work independently much of the time. People who are self-directed (and don't mind spending hours in collection storage) are best suited for this job.
- Registrars certainly develop transferable skills on the job. However, as most people outside of the museum field don't fully understand what a registrar does, finding a non-museum job, if the need arises, will require explaining how the skills transfer.

COLLECTIONS MANAGER

In many museums, collection managers and registrars are one in the same: it may be a "slash" title ("registrar/collections manager") or the person may have a hybrid job that takes one title or the other, without recognizing the distinction. There *is* a distinction, however, and these roles will be separate jobs in very large and jumbo museums. When the jobs are separate, the registrar manages the data related to the collection, whereas the collections manager has an even more hands-on role in managing the collection and maintaining its physical condition per field-wide best practices. This may mean making custom storage containers for fragile objects, monitoring the readings on climate-control data monitors, or keeping track of when light-sensitive objects like prints or documents need to be rotated out of the galleries.

If the museum has a conservation department, the collections manager will work closely with the conservation staff. If there is no conservator on staff, or if the staff conservators don't have expertise in a particular type of object, the collections manager will engage outside conservators as necessary and oversee their work. The collections manager also collaborates with curators and exhibitions staff (discussed in the next chapter) to assist when collection objects are going on view. Examples of such tasks include moving objects out of storage into the galleries, performing routine cleaning of objects or galleries, sewing a hanging sleeve onto the back of a textile, or preparing objects for review by the collections committee. Like the registrar, the collections manager uses the collections database to record all actions that have been taken with objects. One distinction of the collections manager's job is that she typically works with the collection owned by the museum, and less frequently—if at all—with loans.

Many of the attributes and skills listed under registrars also apply to collections managers. They must be adept at using databases and meticulous in recordkeeping. In addition, a job as a collections manager may be a good fit for a person who:

- Wants to spend more time with objects than sitting behind a desk
- Is good at establishing and following procedures
- Believes that the proper handling of objects leaves absolutely nothing to chance
- Prioritizes the safety of the objects above all else, even if this means sacrificing efficiency or having to enforce policies with other staff

- Has a profound appreciation for the physicality and uniqueness of objects; simply put, loves objects and the stories they tell
- Likes to be behind the scenes: this is a wear-jeans-to-work job most days

Skills and experience that may help a candidate get hired as a collections manager (in addition to skills listed under registrars):

- Extreme care and conscientiousness
- Ability to work collaboratively in a small team
- Problem-solving skills
- A BA or equivalent (such as a bachelor of science or of fine arts)

ARCHIVIST

An archivist's role has much in common with a curator's; the distinction is that an archivist works primarily with documents rather than with objects. An archive is essentially a type of library that houses unique or rare documents. In different types of museums, the archive serves distinct functions. In a museum with a collection of art, objects, artifacts, specimens, or living collections, the archive might contain historical documents related to the institution. In this case, the archive may be combined with the library, and its holdings are not considered part of the collection.

In other museums, such as historical societies or museum/library hybrids, like presidential libraries, the archive *is* the collection; these institutions have more in common with museums than with public or university libraries. In these cases, the archivist may take on a role that closely aligns with our description of curator earlier in this chapter.

While libraries and archives have some similarities, one key difference is that archives contain rare documents of historical significance, which are retained in perpetuity. Libraries may have some rare books in a subset of the collection that functions as an archive, but for the most part, library materials are readily available and are retained only for their useful life. In an archive, damaged materials will be treated, when possible, by document conservators, whereas in a library they would be discarded and replaced if still relevant.[6]

Archivists in archive-focused museums research objects, write about them, and create displays and exhibitions to share them with the public. Archivists also assess materials for purchase or donation to the collection. In any type of museum that employs an archivist, one of the primary duties includes working with researchers, both in-house (other staff who need to use the material) and from the public. Access to archives is usually limited, granted only upon review of an application and only to individuals who are actively engaged in research, such as writing a dissertation. The archivist assists researchers in locating and accessing materials. Oftentimes researchers share their final products, such as copies of publications, with the archive as a way to supplement the ongoing research about the collection.

An archivist working in a curatorial role at a large or jumbo institution may oversee an assistant or associate archivist. An archivist occupying more of a librarian role may be the only one on staff.

A job as an archivist might be a good fit for a person who:

- Has expertise in a particular content area represented in the archive
- Is a skilled researcher
- Knows how to appropriately handle rare and possibly fragile materials
- Enjoys not only originating research but also assisting others with theirs

Skills and experience that may help a candidate get hired as an archivist:

- Internships, apprenticeships, or work experience with collections, object handling, or conservation
- Database experience
- Customer service (especially any highly individualized customer service)
- A master's in a relevant content area, in archival studies, or in library and information science; some institutions may prefer a PhD

PROFILE

Christina Bulow, Assistant Curator, Pearl Harbor Aviation Museum, Ford Island, Hawaii

Christina Bulow
Courtesy of Christina Bulow

Christina has a hybrid role that combines several of the positions discussed in this chapter.

"As assistant curator, I fill the role of registrar, collections manager, and assistant curator all in one. I am in charge of the physical condition and security of the collection; am responsible for the accuracy and completion of loan, accession, and deaccession records; and aid in the curation and development of physical and online exhibits."

Christina's background is a bit unconventional, exemplifying the fact that many different paths can lead to museum work.

I have a BA in history, which gives me a knowledge of general history, research, and historical methods. I completed my MA in museum studies at the University of Leicester, which gives me a firm grasp on theory and practice of all areas of the museum profession. I gained valuable skills and insights through a series of volunteer and contract positions following the completion of my MA. Unable to find a 'real' museum job within a few years, I joined the military to gain real world leadership experience and the coveted veteran's preference for federal museum jobs. With every small job I took in the meantime, I looked for valuable museum skills. For example, substitute teaching gave me classroom and lesson experience. Having spent years between earning my degrees and nabbing that first real museum job, I was surprised how many skills from even part-time jobs or the military could roll over into museums.

Her favorite and least favorite parts of her job? "I love working with the artifacts and photographs and learning small histories. The paperwork and backlog are not even that bad, if time-consuming and confusing. However, the frustrating part is advocating for your collection. Sometimes you have to watch other priorities, trivial or extravagant, get attention over things like storage space and environment improvements."

Christina understands the challenge of looking for museum work and advocates remaining as flexible as possible:

That awful catch-22 of needing experience for a job but needing the job for experience is frustrating. Just keep volunteering until you get your foot in the door. Don't be afraid to apply for a variety of positions. Even though we have our preferred areas of museums, maintain skills in other areas. You never know when you need them. I was hired in my current position when I applied for an educator role. The director saw my experience and asked if I would take an unadvertised vacancy.

6

Exhibitions

A well-designed exhibition often interacts so seamlessly with the objects it displays that visitors don't even notice the design itself. What they do notice, however, are the *effects* of the expertly executed design: the story of the exhibition unfolds at just the right pace; objects installed on opposite walls seem to be having a conversation with each other; subtle lighting draws attention to details we otherwise would have missed; carefully chosen paint colors subtly delineate the thematic sections of the exhibition; signage ties into the mood of the exhibition without distracting from the objects. While these elements might appear effortless, each is the result of planning and execution carried out by a skilled team of practitioners in the exhibitions department.

In last chapter's discussion, we made a distinction between exhibitions and collections in terms of curators and registrars: we talked about exhibitions as usually being time-limited and collections displays as more permanent. When we talk about the exhibitions department, though, that distinction isn't necessary—in this case, "exhibition" means any instance in which objects are placed in the gallery spaces (or similar public spaces) to be viewed. The term could refer to a major exhibition that spans multiple galleries and includes dozens of objects, or it could refer to a single object or display case.

A side note: in my experience, many people who work in exhibitions departments are also artists. These jobs tend to be a good fit for their visual sense, familiarity with a variety of materials, and comfort with objects that are fragile or otherwise require special care. These artists/exhibitions team members undoubtedly also find inspiration and camaraderie in the museum environment.

EXHIBITION DESIGNER

The exhibition designer works with the curator to conceptualize the physical environment of the exhibition. In planning an exhibition, the curator determines its thesis and narrative, selects the objects, and usually has a sense of the organization of the space, especially if an exhibition is divided into sections or follows a chronology. The exhibition designer and the curator begin to work together several months before an exhibition opens, allowing plenty of time for planning and fabrication of any required exhibition elements. Additionally, the design may play a role in the "branding" of an exhibition, meaning that other museum departments—such as marketing and the museum shop—need a preview early enough for their advanced planning.

Once the curator establishes a vision, the exhibition designer will use one of several methods to begin to mock up the show. Depending on personal preference and institutional needs, options include three-dimensional design software, a two-dimensional drawing program, or a scale model of the gallery. The designer will begin to plot scale thumbnails of the objects into the mock-up to get a sense of how they will fit into the space. Considerations at this stage include not only the curator's narrative, but also the height or weight of objects, their light restrictions, or the power supply required for a technology component. For exhibitions that will attract large crowds, or that have "must-see" objects, the designer will think about crowd flow and potential bottlenecks. For exhibitions anticipating large numbers of school groups, the designer needs to allow space for them to gather and possibly to sit on the floor or on stools in view of key objects. The designer may also consult with the education team, security, information technology staff, and other colleagues whose input may influence the final design. For example, the education team may be planning a hands-on interactive that needs to be located in a quiet corner of the gallery; the designer will take that into account.

After the basic flow of an exhibition is determined (or as a simultaneous process) the designer, again in collaboration with the curator, creates the "feel" of an exhibition—its "brand," to put it another way—using elements including wall colors, graphics and signage, cases, lighting, furniture, and video monitors; the exact elements will depend, of course, on the particulars of the project. For example, an exhibition intended for families may have brightly colored walls, reading corners with beanbags and area rugs, playful graphics, easy-to-read signage, large-scale cutouts for photo opportunities, and objects hung at a child-friendly height. An exhibition of artifacts from ancient Egypt might have dramatic lighting, sand-colored walls, diagrams of the inside of a pyramid, and the title on the wall in gold vinyl to echo the paint on a sarcophagus.

When the exhibition has been fully conceptualized, the designer works with the rest of the exhibitions team and with outside vendors to bring the vision to life. Careful planning is necessary to ensure that the galleries are closed to the public for the shortest possible time. This is especially true with temporary exhibitions that occupy a dedicated space; while these exhibitions draw visitors, the crowds, and the related income they bring, typically slow down during the period between exhibitions.

As mentioned in the curator section, even the most rigorously planned exhibition needs to allow for some adjustments to occur once the designer and the curator are in the physical space with all the objects. This process can't be replicated with any kind of planning tool and is often the factor that gives an exhibition its spark.

A job as an exhibition designer may be a good fit for a person who:

- Can visualize a three-dimensional space based on a thematic concept
- Is comfortable with different methods of visual planning, including various software as well as low-tech methods
- Is a leader: an exhibition designer needs to coordinate a team of people, including both colleagues and outside vendors or contractors
- Works well under pressure: exhibitions are often installed on a tight timeline and may have unforeseen delays
- Doesn't mind getting their hands dirty: exhibition designers' jobs often overlap with preparators' (see the following) especially at small museums.

Skills and experience that may help a candidate get hired as an exhibition designer:

- Any kind of design experience (even in fields like interior design or event design)
- Computer skills
- Object handling experience
- Carpentry or other types of building/fabricating experience
- A BA or BFA is likely required; an MA or MFA may be preferred

Keep in mind:

- The workload may ebb and flow depending on the exhibition schedule; there might be relatively quiet periods followed by a frenzied few weeks before a show opens.
- An exhibition designer has to be quick on his feet to deal with issues like this real-life example: an object's measurements were miscalculated by a quarter of an inch, so the object does not fit through the gallery door.
- Though the exhibition designer and the curator are equal partners in creating a beautiful exhibition, the curator will undoubtedly be its public face. Depending on the designer's preference for being in the spotlight (in my experience, most of them are comfortable behind the scenes), this might be frustrating or it might be a relief.

PREPARATOR

Most people outside of the museum field have not heard the term preparator. Indeed, as I write this, spell check has underlined each instance of the word with a red squiggle. Even so, we can easily deduce the word's meaning: someone who prepares. In this case, the preparator readies the elements of an exhibition and she implements the exhibition designer's plan. To highlight some of the preparator's tasks, let's imagine a museum with a dedicated temporary exhibition gallery and a schedule that allows for three weeks between exhibitions. In this case, a preparator would start by deinstalling the exhibition that has just closed to the public. This entails removing objects from walls and cases and working with the collections manager and registrar to either return the objects to collection storage or pack them up to be returned to a lender. Next, the preparator deinstalls all of the support material (labels, vinyl signage, cases, furniture, interactives, etc.); these are either returned to storage, returned to the relevant department, or discarded or recycled.[1] If the gallery has moveable walls or panels, the preparator will reconfigure those elements according to the design of the upcoming exhibition. Often, the space is repainted for the next exhibition, depending on time and budget (repainting a gallery can cost several thousands of dollars); an outside contractor may do the painting in order to facilitate a quick turnaround.

To install the new exhibition, this process takes place in reverse: first, the objects are brought into the space. The exhibition designer and curator confirm the layout, and the preparator installs the work on the walls, in cases, on stands, or otherwise according to the exhibition design. If the exhibition features the work of a contemporary artist, especially if it is installation-based and/or site-specific, the preparator will help assemble the artwork per the artist's instructions. In these cases, preparators have to be able to work with an almost unfathomable range of materials. In my personal experience as an assistant curator, I worked on contemporary art installations for which the preparators had to handle many diverse and challenging materials: extremely delicate webs of lampworked glass suspended from the ceiling, an inch-thick layer of dried rose petals carpeting the gallery floor, and an installation composed of stacked refrigerators, to name just three examples.

The preparator then hangs all of the signage, arranges gallery furniture, and works with other staff to perfect the aspects of the exhibition that they oversee. For example, an educator may collaborate with the preparator to install a children's area; an information technology or audio/visual specialist might call on the preparator to help install monitors or other equipment; security staff might work with the preparator to place security barriers in front of objects that require them.

As these examples suggest, preparators work in teams out of necessity; many parts of the job, such as installing heavy or large objects, cannot be performed alone. At large or jumbo museums, there will typically be a team of preparators, because the gallery spaces are large, and because several galleries may be changing over at once. If there is only one preparator, that person will work with curatorial staff on the aspects of the exhibition that require multiple pairs of hands. At small or mid-size museums, the exhibition designer and preparator roles may be combined into one position. At micro and small museums, preparators may work as contractors rather than being on staff.

While the most intense part of the preparator's job comes when exhibitions change over, other ongoing tasks take place as well. Like all exhibition staff, preparators are usually simultaneously working on several exhibitions with different lead times: say, contracting the painters for an exhibition opening next quarter, meeting with an artist whose installation takes place in six months, or problem solving with a curator about how to install some particularly fragile objects in an exhibition still in the early planning stages. Preparators also have ongoing work outside of exhibitions, such as assisting the collections manager in rotating light-sensitive materials out of the galleries, or staging potential acquisitions for a collections committee meeting.

A job as a preparator may be a good fit for a person who:

- Wants an active, hands-on position with as little desk time as possible
- Works well in a team
- Is exacting and detail-oriented
- Has the strength and dexterity to lift and handle heavy or bulky objects (e.g., art or artifacts as well as display cases)
- Is an inveterate problem solver
- Enjoys a wide variety of tasks, from moving objects to painting walls to working with artists

Skills and experience that may help a candidate get hired as a preparator:

- Past work as a contractor, carpenter, builder, or mover
- Object handling experience
- A team-oriented attitude
- Basic office-related computer skills
- Educational background will vary quite a bit, from high school graduates to people with college degrees or MFAs

Keep in mind:

- This is a very physical job; people considering a long-term career as a preparator may want to think about how their ability to manage the physical activities might change as they age, or if they were to get injured.
- Most preparators are men (though not our profilee in this chapter!); women in this field could feel isolated.
- Unless they work at a large or jumbo museum, preparators may need to work as a contractor for several museums in order to earn the equivalent of a full-time salary; in that case, they would need to be comfortable being self-employed and handling tasks like bidding for jobs, invoicing, purchasing insurance, and scheduling.

MOUNT MAKER

Very large and jumbo museums often have mount makers on staff. Mounts are custom-made display mechanisms—stands, holders, and the like—that have two primary functions: they allow objects to be seen as the curator intends, and they ensure that objects are secure when they are on display. Mounts can be constructed of a variety of materials, including metal, wood, Plexiglas, or even fabric. For example, if a curator wants to show a manuscript and keep it open to a particular page, the mount might consist of a wooden bookstand and delicate fabric straps that keep the book open. Or, a curator may want to hang a group of ancient coins in a wall case; because the coins are different sizes, each requires custom-made prongs to attach it to the back of the case. Perhaps some of the coins will be positioned on the deck of the case, angled with tiny mirrors behind them so viewers can see their versos.

A mount maker is a craftsperson: each mount is both a work of art and a feat of engineering. He has to be skilled in working with a wide variety of materials to create mounts with two key characteristics: they have to be unobtrusive so as not to compete with or distract from the objects, and they need to be safe for the objects—material must be archival, and any part of a rigid mount that touches an object needs to be cushioned.

Some museums use custom mounts only for objects that are particularly tricky to display or are an unusual size or shape and use commercially available mounts or stands for other objects that are less finicky; objects without unique requirements may not need mounts at all in some institutions. On the other hand, some museums use mounts for *all* objects on view. This is the case, for example, for museums in earthquake-prone areas; all objects must be secured to minimize damage in the case of an earthquake.

In small and mid-size museums, mount maker is not a separate position but is instead subsumed into another role either in the curatorial or in the exhibitions department. Micro and very small museums typically use off-the-shelf mounts from an exhibition supply company, and only contract with a mount maker in rare circumstances.

A job as a mount maker may be a good fit for someone who:

- Wants to apply skills as an artist or craftsperson to a museum setting
- Is a creative problem solver
- Can both work on a team (with the curator, exhibition designer, preparator, and/or collections manager) and independently
- Is meticulous in their work

Skills or experience that may help a candidate get hired as a mount maker:

- Extensive experience working with metal, wood, Plexiglas, and other materials
- Art, design, or professional craft experience
- Engineering experience

- Object handling
- Familiar with safety standards and procedures in a studio or shop setting
- Educational background will vary, as with preparators; mount makers may train in an apprenticeship model

Keep in mind:

- Relatively few museums have mount makers on staff, and those that do are typically very large or jumbo and located in metropolitan areas; this could limit flexibility if a person needed to move for a non-job-related reason.
- This is an extremely specialized job. Positions may be hard to find; conversely, highly skilled mount makers might be sought after when openings do occur.
- The specialization may lead to feelings of professional isolation; mount makers will need to be proactive in finding colleagues and keeping up to date with technical skills.
- While there are certainly opportunities to work in teams, mount makers spend much of their time in their studio or shop.

PROFILE

Margo Lentz-Meyer, Art Handler, Institute of Contemporary Art, Richmond, Virginia

Margo Lentz-Meyer
Courtesy of Margo Lentz-Meyer

Margo holds two part-time jobs at different museums (she is also a processing archivist at the Virginia Museum of Fine Arts in Richmond, Virginia), which is unfortunately not an uncommon situation among museum staff, as many museums lack the budget to create full-time positions for roles that are not required on a daily basis. For this profile, we'll focus on the art handler job, though Margo's comments also touch upon the archives role. While this chapter does not include a position with the exact title of art handler, Margo's description of her work aligns closely with the description of the preparator job discussed previously. She is one of the relatively rare women working in this role.

Margo says,

I work with a team of about eight guys to de-install and install exhibitions at the Richmond, Virginia, Institute for Contemporary Art. Growing up I had a lot of experience in wood shops and working with general carpentry tools because my dad is a general contractor. During the summers I would paint houses and work on small house renovation projects with him, and later with friends. This experience combined with my archives experience helped me get a job as an art handler.

Margo goes on to explain what surprised her about the job, and what she particularly likes and dislikes about it:

> Working as an art handler and installer at a contemporary art museum, there is a lot of fabrication work that goes into each show, as opposed to simply unpacking, hanging, and repacking that goes into exhibitions at most fine art museums. What was surprising is how much I still need to learn about audiovisual equipment. Audio installation can be quite complicated.[2] My favorite part about working at the [Institute of Contemporary Art] is that I get to handle art, and see the full cycle of an exhibition from blank walls and art in crates, to opening receptions, and back to taking it all down and packing it up again. My least favorite part of the job is doing the final layout with the curators because it can be a lot of standing around trying very hard to both stay out of the way and stay engaged.

Margo offers these insights to prospective art handlers and preparators:

> Get as many internships and part-time positions as you are able while you are in school; that experience will be invaluable. While I was in grad school I was a full-time student, had one part-time job at the California State Parks Archives, and each semester took an unpaid internship. I know that is not possible for everyone, but it allowed me to graduate from the program in two years with a lot more experience than many of my classmates. Be patient and be persistent. If there aren't any internships available at an institution where you want to work, see if someone will create one for you, or volunteer to get your foot in the door. It might not lead to a job but you will begin to network and see what the job really is. It's not always very glamorous.

She also emphasizes the changing role of information technology in museums:

> Right now there is a lot of effort to digitize museum collections, and to add more digital and interactive components to exhibitions. I think that trend will only continue to grow and expand. Having a solid foundation in computing languages, digital asset management systems, and [information technology] infrastructure is going to become increasingly important for museum employees from curators to visitor services.

7

Conservation

"Conservator" is another title, along with curator, that may be familiar even to people who are not regular museumgoers. Though conservators work behind the scenes, the fact that they work directly with objects makes their job seem fairly straightforward. In reality, though, conservation is a highly competitive and multifaceted field. Of all the museum jobs that appear in this book, the path to becoming a conservator is the most rigid. Almost every other museum job has multiple pathways to entry, but conservators must complete a rigorous and prescribed training process. Conservation training programs are highly selective, and preparing the requirements can be grueling. The benefit of the selectivity, though, is that people who complete the process are likely to find jobs. The conservation field is small and interconnected; it's hard to break into, but opportunities abound after passing the initial hurdles.

One of the reasons that conservation is a rigorous specialty is that it combines two fields: chemistry and history or art history. Developing expertise in both of these areas requires extensive time, hard work, and resources. These fields don't naturally overlap in an academic setting: college requirements for chemistry likely won't coincide with those for history or art history. Therefore, students who are interested in conservation as a field need to plan their coursework from an early stage of their college careers to make sure they can fit all the requirements into their schedules.

CONSERVATOR

Conservators are highly specialized professionals who restore, repair, and perform preventative maintenance on works of art and artifacts. Let's take a moment to look more closely at each of those terms. When a conservator *restores* an object, the goal is to bring it as close as possible to its original state. This may entail cleaning the object, filling in some missing paint, or removing past restorations that were not performed correctly or have deteriorated over time. A *repair* counteracts the damage that an object has suffered for one of several reasons: age or insect infestation; accidental mishandling or breakage; or damage from natural disasters. *Preventative maintenance* refers to the process of addressing a non-urgent condition issue to prevent further deterioration over time. For example, flaking paint on a canvas may be "consolidated" (adhered to the support) to make additional loss less likely to occur.

Though it may seem like a timeless process, conservation has undergone an evolution of best practices as technology has advanced. Conservators must actively pursue ongoing professional education to remain up to date on best practices as they continue to evolve. One of the core principles of the field dictates that, to the extent possible, all treatment must be reversible (able to be removed); this reversibility leaves the door open for more effective techniques that might be developed later. Further, the materials used must be distinguishable from the object's original materials, so as to prevent any possible confusion about which portions of the object are original.[1] While the safety of the object is the first priority, another concern is to minimize the distraction that a damaged area might create for the viewer. For example, if a painting has lost some surface paint but the object is not otherwise damaged, the conservator may choose to fill in that lost area with a similar tone of paint. The conservator will do the minimum intervention necessary to eliminate the distraction. For instance, if the paint loss was on a leafy tree in a landscape, the conservator would not try to re-create the leaf pattern but would instead fill in the area with a flat color that closely matched its surroundings. These are just a few examples of the many decisions conservators must make about the appropriate treatment of objects, based on best practices, consultations with colleagues, and their own experience and judgment.

Relatively few museums have conservation departments; those that do are typically large or jumbo. Museums on the smaller side of that range may have one conservator, whereas larger museums may have an entire division with several conservators. For example, the Getty Museum has one of the nation's foremost conservation programs, with four departments and twenty-five conservators and associated staff.[2] Conservators usually specialize in working with a particular type of material: paper (prints, drawings, photographs, books, maps, manuscripts, and so forth), paintings, textiles, and objects are the main categories. Note that while we have been using the term "object" to refer to any work of art or artifact in a museum, in the context of conservation "object" refers specifically to a three-dimensional work of art or artifact. To avoid confusion, we'll continue to use our broader definition of "object" and use the term "artifact" to refer to the category of three-dimensional objects treated by conservators.

Those general categories can be further subdivided, depending on the parameters of the museum's collection. An archive might have multiple paper conservators, each of whom specializes in a different type of material. Paintings conservators might specialize by medium or time period. Artifact conservators might further specialize by material—glass, ceramic, metal, or even plastic.

Because relatively few museums have conservation departments, those that do may serve as a regional conservation center for other museums in the area: museums without conservation staff can contract with museum conservation labs in their area and send objects to them for treatment. Not only does this practice make conservation services available to more museums, but it also generates earned income for the museums that carry out the treatment. Many conservators work independently, especially those that are highly specialized. Even museums that do have conservation departments will send objects out to independent conservators for treatment if those objects are outside of the staff conservators' areas of expertise.

Conservators spend their time in a variety of ways. Some of their work is administrative: writing condition reports and treatment plans, managing junior staff, preparing departmental budgets, and so forth. Assessment of objects is another key task: a curator may consult with a conservator about the condition of an object being proposed as an acquisition for the museum, or a conservator may weigh in on whether an object requested as a loan to another museum can travel safely. If the department works with other museums or private individuals (as some do, as an additional source of earned income), conservators will examine objects to determine if they are good candidates for treatment, and, if so, to prepare estimates.

The other part of the conservator's job—the one that comes to mind when most of us picture a conservator at work—takes place in the conservation studio or lab: the actual hands-on treatment of an object. Regardless of what specific type of treatment is required, restoring, repairing, or performing preventative maintenance on an object is a painstaking process that requires expertise in the tools, materials, and processes, as well as a steady hand. Conservators work with irreplaceable objects and must be calm, confident, and careful—not unlike a surgeon in an operating room. Treatment may be relatively quick, or it may be very slow: if the treatment is especially arduous but not particularly risky—say many days or weeks of cleaning a painting—a junior member of the team may carry out the process.

Conservators must know how a particular object will react to the selected treatment. To have command of this knowledge, conservators need to understand how to use various solvents, paints, adhesives, or specialized materials like gold leaf. They must also know enough about the object and its context to be able to make sound assumptions and decisions about the best way to care for it. For example, before treating a manuscript, a conservator needs to know—or find out—key information about it: where and when it was made, the type of materials used in that time and place, and what clues exist about the author's style and intent. This information may be in the object's database record, or the conservator (often in concert with the curator) must perform research or make an educated guess if no documentation is available. A variety of tools and diagnostic processes can help with this analysis: microscopes, ultraviolet lights, and even x-rays.

Prospective conservators must follow a specific protocol to prepare for training. The website for the American Institute for Conservation of Historic and Artistic Works (AIC) (conservation-us.org) lists only eight graduate degree programs. Each of those programs accepts only a small number of students each year. To be eligible to apply, students must have met certain undergraduate requirements and have had either an internship or an assistantship in a conservation department. A portfolio of conservation work from the internship or assistantship is required to apply to graduate school. Even after completing a two- to four-year graduate degree, conservators may be expected to work in a post-graduate position before applying for full conservator positions. To reiterate a point from the beginning of this chapter, conservator is the only position within museums that requires a specific type of training and degree; other jobs have a wider range of acceptable credentials. For example, curators might have MAs or PhDs, and they can come from many fields—history, art history, science, archaeology, or another related discipline. Educators might be former classroom teachers or have degrees similar to curators'. These examples can be extrapolated to any other department in the museum, outside of conservation.

Because of the apprenticeship model that the conservation field uses, virtually all full conservators occupy some type of teaching role. This role takes different forms: one-on-one mentoring, working with small groups of interns or apprentices, or even, primarily in university museums, teaching formal courses. The apprenticeship model and the emphasis on internships and work experience create a close-knit field with a strong professional network.

A job as a conservator may be a good fit for a person who:

- Is equally interested both in chemistry and in history, art history, archaeology, or another related field
- Has the time, resources, and desire to pursue rigorous graduate work, internships, and apprenticeships
- Is meticulous, detail-oriented, and good with their hands
- Remains calm under pressure
- Can work as part of a team as well as independently
- Can concentrate on one project for long periods of time
- Enjoys mentorship and teaching, whether informal or formal

Skills and experience that may help a candidate get hired as a conservator:

- Project management
- Writing skills

- Public speaking skills (though much of conservators' work is behind the scenes, they do often give lectures and presentations on their work)
- Teaching experience
- Knowledge of safety and occupational health standards (relevant because of the chemicals conservators often use)
- Specific educational requirements for conservators can be found at the AIC website, conservation-us.org

Keep in mind:

- As described, the field is quite competitive, and the number of museums with staff conservators is limited. Therefore, conservators tend to have a lot of longevity at their institutions; while this is in many ways a perk, it also means that there may be little flexibility in terms of relocating.
- To have more flexibility, prospective conservators should consider whether, at some point in their careers, they would be comfortable working as a consultant, and taking on the small business tasks this requires.

CONSERVATION TECHNICIAN

A conservation technician is a museum employee who assists with the conservator's work, perhaps as a precursor to applying to a conservation graduate program for further training. A technician works on objects under a conservator's direct supervision; in fact, graduate programs may require that candidates have a certain number of documented hours of directly supervised work. Technicians may set up materials, prepare projects, ready objects for treatment, and may perform some types of treatments themselves. Often the treatments that technicians perform on their own are less invasive than those performed by conservators—cleaning, for instance, or stitching a support fabric to the back of a textile. Following the apprenticeship model, the technician's responsibilities are likely to increase over time and with practice.

If the conservation department accepts objects from the public or from other museums, the conservation technician might be the first point of contact for such inquiries. In a sense, the relationship between a conservation technician and a conservator is not unlike that between a physician's assistant and a physician. The physician's assistant initially screens the patient; carries out preliminary procedures like taking blood pressure, pulse, and medical history; and then briefs the doctor on the patient's needs. Armed with this information, the doctor examines the patient, determines a treatment plan, and, depending on the type of treatment, either performs it himself (surgery as an obvious example), directs the assistant to follow up (e.g., explaining home care instructions), or sends the patient to another colleague (an x-ray technician or a specialist). Similarly, the conservation technician will carry out many aspects of the conservation assessment and treatment; the conservator makes the final decision about the object's needs and performs the "surgery"—the parts of the treatment that require more specialized expertise.

Both conservation technicians and full conservators often work closely with collections managers and collections care staff. In many museums, especially small ones, these positions are merged: the collections manager will perform some conservation tasks, though full conservation treatment is likely to be sent out to contract conservators.

Though some technicians may occupy the position as a precursor to graduate school, others may have determined that graduate school is not a good fit for them, and instead pursue a technician position as an alternate way to work in the field rather than as a path to a conservator job. Either reason for seeking out a technician job is equally valid; it's a personal choice.

A job as a conservation technician may be a good fit for a person who:

- Wants to become a conservator and needs experience for graduate school applications
- Or, conversely, knows (or needs to confirm) that they don't want to fulfill the requirements for a full conservator position for any number of reasons, yet still wants to put skills and interest in chemistry and history (or a related field) to work
- Is meticulous and highly attuned to detail
- Enjoys working with the public and colleagues as well as independently

Skills and experience that may help a candidate get hired as a conservation technician:

- Art or object handling
- Studio or shop experience in art, craft, design, fabrication, or related fields
- Understanding of hazardous material regulations
- Lab experience
- Recordkeeping and database work
- Public speaking or customer service
- Educational requirements depend on the technician's goals. A BA will be required; technicians working toward full conservator status will need to follow portfolio and other requirements listed on the AIC website, conservation-us.org

Keep in mind: While neither of the motivations for coming to this job—on the way to a full conservator job, or instead of one—is more legitimate than the other, there is a definite hierarchy within conservation. Therefore, it is important to understand that a technician position is not a shortcut to becoming a full conservator.

FRAMER

Very large and jumbo museums that frequently display works on paper (prints, photographs, or drawings) may have a framer on staff. While the particulars of this job are probably easy for any reader to imagine and don't require a great deal of explanation, I wanted to highlight a job in the conservation field—broadly defined—that has a lower bar for entry and is also transferable outside of museums. A job as a framer can provide an opportunity to get a first-hand look at the inner workings of a conservation department, which can be useful, for example, before deciding whether to pursue a graduate degree. It's also a job with quite a bit of flexibility, and it might be a good fit for an artist or to supplement a part-time job at a gallery or frame shop.

Museum visitors may not realize that most works on paper are stored unframed in collection storage to save space. These works are typically stored in mats to protect them from being bent or otherwise damaged and covered with archival paper to protect the surface from scratches and from light. When a curator selects unframed works on paper for an exhibition, the framer will place them in whatever type of stock frame the museum prefers. A collections manager may also perform this task, which is likely the case at small to mid-size museums.

A job as a museum framer may be a good fit for a person who:

- Wants to work in a hands-on capacity with objects
- Likes the environment of a conservation setting but has decided not to pursue a conservation track
- Is extremely careful, conscientious, and attentive to detail
- Is an artist or has another related job or skill that they want to supplement

Skills and experience that may help a candidate get hired as a museum framer:

- Experience as an artist, in a gallery, in an art supply store, or in a frame shop
- Excellent technical skills with various tools and framing materials (mats, metal or wood, and glass)
- Precision in measuring and cutting (e.g., sewing skills are relevant here)
- No particular degree is required, though a BFA or MFA will give a candidate an edge; hands-on experience is essential

Keep in mind:
- A framer position is quite likely to be part-time and without benefits.
- Hours may be irregular, with more intense periods before exhibitions open.
- This job may be a good way for a person with appropriate skills to try out the museum field.

PROFILE

Ingrid A. Neuman, Museum Conservator, Rhode Island School of Design Museum, Providence, Rhode Island

Ingrid Neuman
Courtesy of Ingrid Neuman

Ingrid is an objects (here meaning three-dimensional artworks) conservator who has been in the conservation field for thirty years. She describes her work and her training:

I am responsible for the preventive care and the stabilization of the three-dimensional collections (sculpture, furniture, frames) at the museum. This includes monitoring any dimensional changes that occur to the art and artifacts as a result of seasonal fluctuations in the environment and how these changes can affect the collections both on exhibit and in storage. I have a bachelor's degree in classics, with a focus on Mediterranean archaeology, including some coursework in ancient languages and also a master's degree in art conservation specializing in three-dimensional objects. Between undergraduate and graduate school, I apprenticed for three years with an art restorer to gain practical experience and to develop a portfolio of conservation treatments for my application to a graduate program in art conservation. At the same time I took art classes to create a portfolio of a variety of artistic techniques. As a graduate student, I undertook paid summer internships which allowed me to gain not only practical museum experience but also to determine which type of museum was the best fit for me. After earning the master's degree, I worked at a museum comprised of small historic houses, a large federal museum, a regional art conservation center, small historical societies, and a larger private museum before I settled on my current position in a university museum, which suits me best. I continue to take art classes every year to keep up with the changes in technology such as 3-D printing, laser-cutting, and vacuum forming as well as more traditional art techniques such as glass blowing and letterpress printing. Knowing about how art is created can better inform you about how to repair the work when it is compromised.

Ingrid goes on to talk about one of her favorite perks of her job, as well as one negative:

I was very pleasantly surprised by how much opportunity there is for a conservator to travel as a courier with the artwork, acting as an ambassador and an advocate for the artwork while it is in transit. It is especially interesting to be able to travel to other museum and gallery venues to learn how the staff there works and performs their respective responsibilities. One down side of the conservation field is the use of solvents; we use many chemicals to make our custom-designed cleaning solutions and adhesives. As I work longer in the field, I wish to reduce my own chemical exposure.

A typical workday for Ingrid might look like this:

I start my day cleaning silver for an upcoming exhibition on American decorative arts. I work with many volunteers whom I have vetted and trained to clean and polish with me. After lunch, I often attend meetings with curators concerning exhibitions, loans, or general collections care issues. Between meetings, I work on other museum objects, researching them, documenting them, cleaning or otherwise stabilizing them for exhibition. I often evaluate artwork that is being considered for acquisition either by purchase or donation. After the workday has officially ended, I try to squeeze in research on the collections and also to write papers for presentation at national and international conferences.

Ingrid offers some advice for people who are interested in the conservation field:

Be perseverant. There is a significant number of academic and practical requirements for entrance into a graduate art conservation program. Some pre-program conservation students lose focus and give up too soon. Be systematic and try to enjoy the process of accumulating the requirements. Think creatively and document all of your artistic work for inclusion into a portfolio to highlight your manual dexterity. Make certain that this is the type of work that brings you pleasure by apprenticing in a conservation studio at a museum or with a conservator in private practice. Don't forget to write thank-you notes—a small but important detail.

Like so many museum staff members, Ingrid cites her coworkers as one of the best things about her job: "Without a doubt, the colleagues with whom I work on a daily basis make my job so interesting and pleasurable. In museum work, the collaborative nature of the staff strengthens the job of each individual. When each museum staff member sees his or her position as a part of a greater whole, the entire museum functions at the highest possible level."

8

Communications

Thus far, we've seen that many teams of talented professionals work together to create exhibitions and programs; to care for collections; to conserve objects; and to ensure a safe, comfortable, and inviting environment for visitors. Without the communications staff, though, very few people would know that these activities are taking place. The communications team creates compelling messages about the museum and ensures that those messages are clear, accurate, and fit with the museum's brand or institutional persona. In a sense, the communications department acts as the public face of the museum.

MARKETING MANAGER

For simplicity, we'll use the terminology of marketing manager for the position described in this section. Keep in mind that the structure within the department will vary. In very large and jumbo museums, there will be many marketing staff members, with the director of marketing at the executive level and associate and assistant marketing staffers implementing the marketing plan. In a small museum, there may be only one marketing staff person who also handles other communication roles as discussed later in this chapter.

At the most basic level, the marketing staff of a museum do what marketing staff do at any business: promote a product to consumers. In the case of museums, the "product" is the museum experience, which includes exhibitions, collections, programs, special events, the shop or café—essentially the visit as a whole. The "consumers" are visitors of all types: individuals, groups, families, students, professionals, and so on. While it may seem a bit gauche to talk about selling the museum experience, keep two things in mind: first, though most museums are non-profit, that fact only describes their tax status; to put it another way, non-profit doesn't mean that museums can't make a profit, only that the profits they do make have to go back into the institution's mission-related functions. Indeed, most museums rely on earned income to remain financially viable. Second, marketing a museum experience is not necessarily an easy sell. It may be hard for those of us who are steeped in museums to imagine, but the average person living in our communities is not predisposed to visit museums.[1] Museums aren't on their radar, for whatever reason; frankly, we don't always make it easy for people to visit, with real or perceived barriers related to schedule, cost, transportation, or simply not feeling comfortable or welcome. For those who do sometimes visit museums, or even who visit them often, museums must compete with an almost endless array of possibilities competing for people's free time and disposable income, from attending a baseball game to binge-watching a show on Netflix. Even highly motivated visitors need to decide which museum to visit, meaning that museums compete (albeit in a friendly way) with each other for visitors' time.

The marketing manager creates messages that reach potential audiences and that stand out among the constant influx of messages we see every day. Beyond just standing out, though, those messages have to go further: they have to explain, in a concise and compelling way, what the museum offers and why it's worth the potential visitor's time and money. This task is relatively straightforward with some types of exhibitions—the "blockbusters," as it were. For example, Egyptian mummies or Claude Monet will resonate with many people as exhibitions worth seeing, whether or not they actually plan to visit themselves. With other exhibitions and collections, the task can be much harder; they can run the risk of being seen as esoteric and simply not relevant to people's lives. For example, the Museum of Russian Icons, where I used to work, is a glorious place to spend an afternoon. The building and the collection wowed nearly everyone who walked through the door. However, unless they have Russian heritage and/or are Orthodox, most people don't know what an icon is and feel that Russian art and history are of little relevance to them. Though it wasn't difficult to win visitors over once they saw what the museum had to offer, getting them to that point was the challenge.

While reaching potential audiences may seem like an uphill battle, museum marketing staff do so successfully, day after day. One of the key reasons that their messages get through despite the obstacles is that, on the whole, museums offer experiences that are unique: the chance to encounter one-of-a-kind objects, visit sites where history happened, try our hands at a new skill or activity, and engage in lifelong learning.

The foundation of the marketing manager's role is to craft the message that will resonate with the target audience: what's the most important information to convey, and what's the most effective way to convey it? In promoting an exhibition, the manager needs to come up with a strategy for advertising it. Several related decisions must be made: determining the key messages (e.g., is this a rare opportunity to see objects on loan from a well-known museum?), selecting the images that best exemplify the exhibition, targeting specific audiences, and assessing the best way to reach that audience (e.g., a family-friendly exhibition might be advertised in a publication geared to parents). The marketing team will get input on these factors from the curators, and then will develop a suite of marketing materials to be used in different ways.

There are several different avenues through which the marketing manager disseminates information about the museum. One avenue is advertising. The marketing manager purchases advertising space in print and online publications. Because advertising is often expensive, researching different media outlets and their audiences will help ensure that the ad will reach the intended demographic. Then, when possible, the manager needs to try to track each ad to determine how many people it reached, and whether its cost was a good investment. Online ads can be tracked through tools like Google Analytics, whereas print ads might rely on the use of a coupon or a special offer that the front desk staff can track when the visitor redeems the offer.

Another way that the marketing manager reaches people is through community outreach, sometimes in conjunction with the education department. For example, the museum might have a booth at a street fair or farmers' market where people can pick up information about the museum, perhaps take part in an art project or hands-on activity, and receive discounted passes to the museum. These events are excellent ways to introduce the museum to people who might not otherwise visit; this type of casual, friendly contact with people in a neutral environment can help generate interest in the museum and counteract any concern that the museum might not be a welcoming place.

The marketing manager also creates the content for the museum's printed collateral: things like brochures, rack cards, newsletters, event postcards, annual reports, and so on. Managing social media accounts is also a significant part of the marketing manager's (or a subordinate's) job, as is responding to posts on online review sites. Though the marketing manager may, in some cases, oversee the museum website, we'll cover that function in chapter 11 when we discuss information technology.

The marketing department is typically responsible for leading branding initiatives in the museum. The brand is made up of many different elements that create the visual identity: the logo, how the name is presented (e.g., initials or a shortened version of a longer name), tagline, colors, fonts, and other similar ways of packaging the museum's message. The marketing department can be thought of as the "keeper" of the brand, which other departments then implement in their own work. If material is not produced in the department, the marketing manager might request the option to approve documents, signs, and other materials produced by colleagues to ensure the brand guidelines have been met.

Another way that marketing helps to make people aware of the museum is to engage with partners in the community to co-advertise and co-sponsor events. For example, the marketing manager may cultivate relationships with the businesses in the neighborhood. A nearby restaurant, for instance, may offer patrons a discount if they show their museum admission ticket; this helps drive business to both the restaurant and the museum, saving visitors a few dollars in the process. The marketing manager may also work with the development team to get advertising space donated or other types of in-kind marketing support; for example, the local newspaper might offer a discount on advertising, or the public transit system may agree to offer advertising space on the side of their buses.

A job as a marketing manager may be a good fit for a person who:

- Believes in the museum's mission and can create messaging that channels that excitement
- Would enjoy the role of museum ambassador, talking about the museum to a wide variety of people at every opportunity (not only to a business contact at a work event but also to the parent sitting next to her at their kids' soccer game)
- Is a great communicator, in person, in writing, online, and by phone
- Enjoys public speaking
- Is a skilled and strategic user of social media
- Is a constant source of creative ideas

Skills and experience that may help a candidate get hired as a marketing manager:

- A background in advertising, sales, or community outreach
- Public speaking experience
- Copywriting experience
- Basic familiarity with (or willingness to learn about) the content of the museum
- Experience in media—newspapers, radio, television, etc.
- Facility with several (if not all) of the most popular social media platforms.
- At the senior level at a large museum, a marketing director likely has an advanced degree (such as an MBA). At a smaller museum or at a junior level, a BA may be adequate.

Keep in mind:

- Marketing is not a nine to five job. As noted, good marketing managers take every opportunity to promote the museum, even on their own time and as they meet people outside of work.
- Marketing managers must be proactive. For example, if a direct mail piece isn't getting the expected response, the manager might need to organize an impromptu email or phone campaign.
- Sometimes, a marketing manager may feel responsible for low attendance at an event or program, when, of course, many other factors also affect the relative success of the museum's public offerings.
- One of the benefits of this position is that the skills are highly transferable to nearly any other type of business. As I've indicated elsewhere, this kind of flex-

ibility may not seem crucial when an employee is in her twenties, without some of the responsibilities that may tie a person to one place (such as a mortgage), but it can be a lifesaver later on.

PUBLIC RELATIONS OFFICER

While marketing and public relations (PR) may be combined into one role in a small museum, in a large, very large, or jumbo museum they are typically separate roles or even separate departments. The main responsibility of the PR manager is to secure press coverage for the museum. Editorial coverage—when news about the museum appears in the press in the form of a review or an article—is extremely valuable to museums. Not only does it draw attention to the work of the museum, but it also does so at no cost to the museum, unlike paid advertising. One of the key ways to garner press interest in the museum's initiatives is through press releases, or documents that provide the key points about a topic in language that the press can use as is or can expand upon as part of a more in-depth story. The PR manager may put multiple press releases together, along with high-resolution images, in a press kit. For exhibitions, press releases are typically sent shortly before the opening to help to build the anticipation for an exhibition.

Journalists receive press releases on a daily basis, and they have to pick and choose which ones to pursue. The PR manager works to build relationships with the press. This allows her to follow up on press releases by sending personal emails or making calls to reporters with whom she has a professional history. PR managers also host in-person events for the press. For example, a few days before an exhibition opens, the PR manager usually invites reporters to the museum to preview the show and to interview the curator, director, or other museum spokesperson.

Though exhibitions may be the focus of many press releases, any newsworthy event at a museum can be the subject: meeting a fundraising goal, hiring a new senior staff person, breaking ground on a building project, or acquiring an important new object for the collection. The PR manager works with the colleague who is in charge of each event to make sure the release covers the most important points.

Above all, the PR manager must be an excellent communicator, able to explain the museum's exhibitions, programs, or other initiatives, in clear and compelling language. The PR manager may serve as the spokesperson for the museum, say if a reporter has a question or requests a statement from the museum's official representative. The PR manager may also be interviewed about museum projects in print, online, or on television or radio. Depending on the topic being covered, the director, board president, or curator may serve as the spokesperson rather than the PR manager. In those cases, the PR manager may act as a coach or advisor if those colleagues are not accustomed to fulfilling a spokesperson role, especially in a crisis situation.

If the museum is involved in some type of a controversy or receives negative press coverage, the PR manager may need to do some damage control by correcting errors, explaining the museum's point of view, or even apologizing on the museum's behalf if necessary. This is perhaps the hardest part of the PR manager's job, especially if the negative press is unexpected.

It may seem strange to dwell on the possibility of negative press or crisis communication, as we don't typically associate museums with a lot of controversy. Though not frequent, negative press or a controversial issue can have an enormous and long-lasting impact on the institution. For example, museums that violate the American Alliance of Museums' code of ethics around deaccessioning may jeopardize future gifts.[2] Malfeasance on the part of the staff or the board can erode public trust, which takes a long time to rebuild. Controversial exhibition topics (be it contemporary art or climate change) can alienate potential visitors who see the exhibition as being in conflict with their personal values. Ability to anticipate and deftly handle these types of issues is a crucial skill of the PR manager.

A job as a PR manager may be a good fit for a person who:

- Communicates with style, particularly in writing and in person (but also over the phone)
- Remains calm under pressure
- Is a genuine people person who is good at building and maintaining professional relationships
- Understands the mission and the work of the museum well, and is able to synthesize information from colleagues on a variety of topics
- Enjoys public speaking, including appearing on live or recorded video or audio
- Can plan ahead but also move quickly in response to an urgent situation

Skills and experience that may help a candidate get hired as a PR manager:

- Excellent writing skills
- Public speaking in any venue
- Experience at a newspaper, television or radio station, or at a news-related website
- Understanding of news cycles, including lead times
- Crisis management training
- Coaching or supervisory experience
- At least a BA, if not an MA or MBA

Keep in mind:

- Work schedules may be unpredictable, depending on what's happening at the museum.
- A crisis, though rare, may pop up at an inconvenient time, and it will need to be handled along with the manager's day-to-day responsibilities.
- This job, like others in the communications department, features highly transferable skills.

- Certain types of museums may be more likely to spark lively debate in the public sphere. Prospective PR managers may want to ask in an interview about the institution's history with handling controversies.

PUBLICATIONS

In some museums the publications department, including editors and graphic designers, reside in curatorial because the majority of content produced takes the form of exhibition texts and catalogs. In other museums, these roles fall under the marketing department because their skills are used primarily for marketing materials. Often, both curatorial and marketing use the services of the publications team, regardless of where the team falls within the organizational chart. In micro and very small museums, one person may shoulder all of these tasks (marketing, PR, and publications). In very large and jumbo museums, there may be separate editors and graphic designers in curatorial and in marketing. Here, I've situated these roles in the communications chapter, but I'll discuss them in a broader museum context. Also, note that here we're talking primarily about printed materials; website management will be covered in chapter 11.

EDITOR

In museums, editors review and revise written material that will be printed in any number of formats: exhibition labels, text panels, and other signage; exhibition catalogs, ranging in scope from brochures to scholarly books; educational material including family guides, teacher packets, and field trip materials; development materials (discussed in more depth in the next chapter) including annual appeal letters, membership brochures and solicitations, annual reports, invitations, and, possibly, grant applications; and marketing and PR materials including ad copy, newsletters, and press releases. Depending on the protocol for generating and reviewing these materials, the editor may be closely involved in the process from the beginning (likely the case for curatorial and marketing materials), or she may serve more of a review role in the final stages, such as proofreading a grant proposal.

The editor often serves as the project manager for printed materials. For example, in the course of mapping out an exhibition, the curator may plan for five text panels, twenty "tombstone" labels (which include only essential information about an object), and ten extended or "chat" labels (which provide more extensive information about selected pieces). Based on this information, and perhaps in consultation with the graphic designer, the editor will determine the required word count and, working backward from the installation date, the timeline and due dates for the draft text, one or two rounds of edits, the final text, review of proofs (full-scale mock-ups of what the final printed piece will look like), and printing.

The editor then acts as the keeper of this schedule, working with the writers (curators, marketing managers, educators, or whoever is the owner of the project) to ensure that they adhere to the schedule. The editor reviews the draft copy, making corrections or suggestions and highlighting areas that need more explanation. A good editor can assume the perspective of the reader, always keeping the intended audience in mind. For example, a scholarly exhibition at a university museum will likely attract an academic audience, meaning that the texts will follow an academic style and may be more dense than would be appropriate for other settings. For a general audience, the editor will be mindful of avoiding jargon and needing to define unfamiliar terminology. For a family audience, the editor will consider the reading levels of the children and which texts might be geared toward adults rather than kids.

In determining the specifications for a particular text, the editor will work closely with the graphic designer. If, for example, the designer and educator have determined that a family guide will be a six-panel brochure with two folds and will include a certain number of images, then the word count for the text will be limited by those parameters. Similarly, to ensure that the text is easy to read and that the labels and panels don't overwhelm the objects in an exhibition, the editor and designer, in consultation with the curator, will determine the physical size of the labels and the font size that is most readable; those factors together determine the length of the text. Often, these specifications are formalized in a house style that stays consistent over time; for example, an extended label may always be designed to measure eight by ten inches and include about one hundred words in sixteen point text. These specifications should follow rules of universal design, ensuring that texts use a font, size, and design that are easy for all audiences—including those with sight impairments—to read.

In managing publication projects, the editor works with outside vendors. Museums on either end of the size spectrum may print material in house to be cost efficient: micro museums may use their office printers because they print on a small scale, whereas jumbo museums may invest in large-format professional printers because they print a large volume of labels and text panels. Museums between these size extremes typically use outside print shops who can produce the labels and text panels at the required size, and who can also print large-volume mailings at a relatively low cost. The editor (or graphic designer) often manages these outside relationships, getting quotes, submitting material to the printer, and approving proofs.

If a museum produces materials in languages other than English, the editor may work with an outside translator (or, depending on her language skills, may translate materials herself). For publications like catalogs, the editor may also manage image permissions required to reproduce photographs in publications.

A job as an editor may be a good fit for a person who:

- Is a good writer
- Has expertise in revising and proofreading texts

- Understands how editing intersects with print production and graphic design
- Works collaboratively
- Can work under tight deadlines
- Knows enough about the museum's content area (or is willing to learn) to be able to work with the terminology and other special considerations

Skills and experience that may help a candidate get hired as an editor:

- Writing, editing, or publishing experience
- Excellent command of English grammar
- Knowledge of the museum's chosen citation style (Chicago Manual of Style, for example)
- Skilled use of relevant software
- Attention to detail
- A portfolio of writing and/or editing work may be required
- At least a BA or BFA (as in creative writing); a MA or MFA may be preferred

Keep in mind:

- This is a job with highly transferable skills.
- The job may be stressful around deadline time.
- Depending on the size of the museum, the position may be part-time, or it may be combined with other positions.
- It's important to establish protocols to make processes efficient (e.g., if a curator completely rewrites a text after it's been edited, the label design process may be derailed).

GRAPHIC DESIGNER

A graphic designer in a museum is responsible for planning and designing the visual aspects of printed material and often online material as well, though the web team may handle that separately. The description of the editor's job goes hand-in-hand with the parameters of the designer's job; essentially all the materials listed for the editor's position go to the graphic designer before or after they go to the editor, or they're designed and edited simultaneously, with the editor and designer working closely together.

Graphic designers use elements like logos, graphics, fonts, colors, illustrations, and photographs to create the visual identity of a piece. Designers are usually closely involved with branding initiatives and work within the guidelines established for the brand across the museum. Designers may create templates that they work within, such as a quarterly newsletter that features the same basic design—with some alterable elements—every time it's printed. Exhibition labels may follow a similar format throughout the museum. Other projects will allow more room for creativity, such as special exhibition signage or other materials, like invitations for openings.

The museum environment seems like the perfect place for a graphic designer, as an artist, to work: there is no shortage of inspiration or visually appealing source material; because, at some level, all museums are based on the appreciation of the visual, museum graphic designers have a high bar to meet, but one that seems like an exciting professional challenge.

Graphic designers work across the museum, in collaboration with any number of different departments. They have to be attuned to the needs of each department's collateral and audiences, and they have to consider the "client's" (their colleague's) vision for the piece while also offering professional input on what design will work best for that particular application. In some museums, graphic designers may also be involved in product design for the museum's retail operation.

A job as a graphic designer may be a good fit for a person who:

- Has a good visual sense in terms of print and/or online materials
- Has prior experience as an artist or designer
- Is able to work collaboratively
- Establishes and adheres to deadlines
- Enjoys or is interested in learning more about the museum's content area
- Wants to work in a creative environment

Skills and experience that may help a candidate get hired as a graphic designer:

- Extensive experience with graphic design software
- Photography and photo editing experience
- A background in art or design
- A portfolio will be required
- A BA or BFA; an MA or MFA may be preferred

Keep in mind:

- A candidate may not have a professional portfolio when applying for a first job, but other projects can be included from school assignments, internships, or extracurricular activities (such as a flyer created for a club).
- The skills a graphic designer uses are highly transferable. Simply put, designers can make more money in the private sector than at a non-profit museum. However, the appeal of a museum's work environment may mitigate the lower pay. It's even possible that a museum will pay graphic designers a relatively high salary (when compared to other staff) to be competitive with the corporate sector.

PROFILE

Gitanjali Jain, Web and Marketing Designer, Tower Hill Botanic Garden, Boylston, Massachusetts

Gitanjali Jain
Courtesy of Kate Wollensak Freeborn

Gitanjali ("Gitu") Jain shares the marketing position at Tower Hill with a colleague who handles the social media and PR aspects of the job. She explains what her role entails:

My job includes marketing and promoting different aspects of Tower Hill Botanic Garden including the educational programs, special events, exhibits, horticulture programs, café, the garden shop, and private events. I manage Tower Hill's website, print marketing, and email marketing and I play an important role in Tower Hill's marketing strategy and brand awareness.

Gitu's background is in design:

I studied graphic design, and took some digital design courses, and always had a profound interest in marketing. I worked as an art instructor before I became a designer. For many years I freelanced, which gave me the wonderful opportunity of working with non-profit organizations, corporations, and individuals. By working with a wide variety of clients, I realized that my passion lies in museums and non-profits and that's why I decided to join the team at Tower Hill Botanic Garden.

One of Gitu's favorite aspects of her job is the variety. She says,

There are so many choices to pursue within digital marketing or print marketing. You get to work on myriad different projects that are equally inspiring and challenging. Looking ahead, digital marketing is going to become even more important. There will be even more ways to reach our audience, but at the same time we will be competing for shorter attention spans. Marketing is a very creative and a wonderful field to be in and I highly recommend it. I absolutely love my work.

While there never seems to be enough time to accomplish everything she wants to, Gitu stays grounded by focusing on the organization's mission:

Some days can feel overwhelming because of the workload. But seeing a happy and inspired visitor makes it all worth it. Tower Hill Botanic Garden enriches the lives of everyone it touches, including visitors, volunteers, and staff. The connection to Tower Hill's mission—to inspire the use and appreciation of horticulture to improve lives, enrich communities and strengthen commitment to the natural world—really helps me stay committed to my role here.

9

Development

Development departments are responsible not only for raising essential funds for the museum, but also for helping to build meaningful relationships with donors. What development staff are developing, essentially, is capacity: the ability for the museum to remain financially stable, and the propensity for individuals, foundations, and corporations to participate in the museum's activities while helping to secure its future.

In the following, to simplify the discussion, I'll talk about managers in various roles, but all of these jobs can be scaled down or up in terms of seniority; that is, jobs in development can range from the assistant to the director level. As is true across the museum, the specifics of the job range with the size of the institution. Micro and small museums typically have one person filling all of the following roles, whereas large, very large, and jumbo museums will have development departments, and even sub-departments, that employ numerous people.

MEMBERSHIP MANAGER

Membership is one of the key ways that a museum builds long-term relationships with its community. At most museums, visitors can purchase memberships that provide free admission and other benefits for a period of one year. Typically, membership falls into two categories. First is standard membership, which offers a basic level of benefits and is designed to pay for itself in two to three visits (that is, the cost of the membership is about equal to the cost of paying admission two or three times). The second major category is philanthropic memberships. These may be purchased at a higher cost; the cost of a regular membership is deducted, and the surplus counts as a donation to the museum. Philanthropic memberships come with additional perks, such as exclusive events or guest passes. For example, if a family membership costs seventy-five dollars per year, a "Family Plus" membership may cost $125 and include the ability to bring a guest on every visit. Philanthropic memberships range in size; at micro and small museums they may cost in the five hundred to one thousand dollar range, whereas at jumbo museums they might cost up to tens of thousands of dollars.

Membership is important for the financial support of the museum, but it is equally important as a reflection of the community's support of the institution. The number of members and statistics like the renewal rate are measures of success that might be considered by granting agencies or even as part of American Alliance of Museums accreditation. The membership manager is responsible for the operation of the membership program. This entails both strategy, such as determining member benefits or organizing members' events, and operations, meaning the administration of the recordkeeping involved with membership. (At a large or jumbo museum, the administrative side of the job is likely to be held by a junior staff member.)

There are many ways that the membership manager cultivates relationships with members. The manager plans and implements enticing membership events, especially opportunities that are available to members only, such as exclusive tours, extended hours, or special exhibition openings. The goal of these events is not only to fulfill the museum's promise to offer membership benefits, but, ultimately to maintain—or, better, grow—the member's commitment to the museum. The best case scenario for museums is that members support the museum well beyond their membership, in any number of ways: introducing friends to the museum, donating to the annual appeal, volunteering at the museum, or even leaving a legacy gift (a gift made through a will after a person's death).

The membership manager works with a large amount of data, usually through some type of a constituent management database that can track members' status and payments. Membership typically operates on an annual cycle, meaning that every month, the manager runs reports in the database to determine who's up for renewal; those people then receive renewal material in the mail or via email. If they don't renew immediately, they typically receive two or three more notices. Attention to detail is key here: records of membership status, contact information, and payments need to be updated on a regular basis.

In addition to maintaining records, the membership manager works with budgets and forecasting, projecting membership income and expense for the upcoming budget cycle. Most of the time, the board and the director expect membership to grow, at least modestly. The manager, then, is responsible for ensuring that it does grow by designing incentives and membership campaigns that help attract more members. In this respect, the membership manager has a sales role.

One of the most important parts of this job is being a people person. In a micro or small museum, the membership manager will likely know nearly all of the members by name. Members join to feel like the museum's extended family, and the manager strives to make this happen.

A job as a membership manager may be a good fit for a person who:

- Loves working with people, especially getting to know them better over time
- Is a meticulous recordkeeper
- Can set and meet ambitious goals
- Sees the value of museum membership and can explain it to prospective members
- Enjoys planning events
- Communicates well in writing, online, and by phone

Skills and experience that may help a candidate get hired as a membership manager:

- Database work (each museum has its preferred software, but any database experience is relevant)
- Payment processing
- Copywriting or advertising experience
- General office skills, including overseeing bulk mailings
- Event planning and implementation
- Sales
- Budgeting
- A BA is likely required with an MA or MBA preferred at large institutions

Keep in mind:

- Jobs in membership are not nine to five. Expect regular evening and weekend hours, as these are the times that members' events typically take place.
- The work is cyclical, both monthly and annually. Some people enjoy this type of structure in the workplace, whereas others crave more variety.
- There may be a significant amount of pressure around goals.
- It's important for a membership manager to remain accessible to members, while also mitigating against frequent interruptions.
- Many other non-profits outside of museums also run membership programs, so the skills of this job are easily transferable elsewhere in the sector.

DEVELOPMENT MANAGER

In departments that are large enough to subdivide into specialties, those specialties are often correlated with the type of constituents that the development managers (also called "officers") focus on. (This is similar to the education department model where staff specialize by audience.) The larger the museum, the more likely it is to have these specialties divided among different managers. There are several main categories of constituents who give to museums. First are individuals. Here, "individual" doesn't necessarily mean a single person (as it typically does in membership), but rather refers to any person or family that is not affiliated with an organization. Corporations often support museums through sponsorships: a company may donate funds to have its name associated with an event or a space at the museum. Corporations may also contribute in-kind goods and services, meaning that the goods and services are provided at no cost to the museum, though their value is considered a corporate donation for tax purposes. Foundations, or non-profit philanthropic organizations, often run by families or the charitable arms of corporations, are another area in which a development manager might specialize. Foundations often give grants through an application process (we'll discuss that more in the grant writer section) but sometimes also give unsolicited gifts in their area of interest. Development managers may also focus on working with government agencies and elected officials to generate support for the organization. In mid-size or large museums with several development managers but without enormous departments, these constituencies may be combined. A typical breakdown in a medium-sized department is for one manager to oversee individual giving and organizational giving, while another oversees corporations, foundations, and government entities.

Sometimes, development managers will specialize by type of gift. Such categories include "major" gifts, legacy or planned giving (gifts made through a person's estate after death), or capital campaign gifts, if the museum is in the process of raising funds dedicated to an expansion, renovation, new building, or other substantial building project.[1]

A development manager's role falls into a few main categories. First is donor relations; this involves skills in relationship building similar to those mentioned previously for the membership manager. Donors to museums rightly expect to be appropriately acknowledged and to have a personal connection to the institution. Though these relationships are not contingent on the size of the donation, major donors receive more perks and the development manager's relationship with them will be more hands on. For example, major donors may offer to host fundraising gatherings at their homes; the development manager will work with the donor to plan and execute the event. A note here: other museum staff may be involved in building relationships with major donors. For example, all board members are expected to make financial gifts to the museum (the minimum board gift amount is usually—but not always—correlated with museum size and stature); the development manager will work closely with the director in procuring these gifts. Curators may also cultivate donors who have substantial private collections of art or objects. In these cases, donations may come in the form of gifts or bequests of objects.

Another key skill of the development manager is knowing whom to ask for donations and for which projects. For example, the development manager will typically know the leadership of the foundations and corporations in the museum's community and will be able to earmark which projects might be a good fit for each foundation's or company's philanthropy. Perhaps a foundation gives most of its charitable dollars to projects that support early childhood initiatives; the development manager might target this foundation as a possible source of funding for a gallery designed for preschoolers. A local food or beverage company might be a candidate to sponsor a fundraising dinner by providing refreshments free or at cost.

One way that development managers keep track of this information is through prospect researching. This is an administrative task, the bulk of which may be carried out by a junior staff member. Basically, prospect researching involves gathering information about individuals, corporations, and foundations, including their interests, past philanthropy, and their capacity for giving (the amount of gift they are thought to be able to afford). Other data may also be collected that might be useful to know for particular projects or initiatives. For example, knowing that a major donor is a graduate of a particular university might be helpful if the museum were to partner with that university on an exhibition or program. In addition to publicly available information, development managers will also keep detailed notes on conversations with donors. Given the importance of collecting detailed information, and using it strategically to solicit funds for projects, the paramount characteristic of a successful development manager is discretion and an unassailable commitment to confidentiality. These are not the museum staff members who will be gossiping around the water cooler, as the success of a development program rests largely on trust.

One key responsibility of development managers is organizing events for donors. These can range in scale and complexity from a simple reception to a gala event. Such events are designed not only to acknowledge existing donors, but also to attract new ones; current donors are often encouraged to bring guests as a way to introduce prospective supporters to the museum.

A job as a development manager may be a good fit for a person who:

- Enjoys meeting people and is highly skilled at cultivating professional relationships
- Understands and can articulate the value of the museum's mission and initiatives
- Is comfortable asking individuals, corporations, and foundations for financial support
- Operates with complete discretion around confidential or personal information
- Is organized, keeps detailed records, and has a good memory for people's names, faces, and interests
- Communicates well in person, in writing, online, and on the phone
- Feels comfortable using a database and handling administrative tasks, like processing payments

Skills and experience that may help a candidate get hired as a development manager:

- Customer service, especially high-end, concierge-level service
- Database skills
- Budgeting and forecasting
- Writing and communications

- Financial management
- At least a BA at entry level; likely an MBA or development certificate at a more senior level or at a larger museum

Keep in mind:

- Expect an irregular schedule, including evenings and weekends.
- Travel may be involved, depending on the reach of the museum and the type of events planned for donors.
- I once saw a job listing for a development position that required "diverse and tireless social skills," which seemed apt. Extroverts—people who are energized by interacting with others—are best suited for this job.
- It's easiest to raise funds for an organization you believe in, so prospective development professionals should take the time to find a good fit.
- In very large and jumbo museums, which are most likely to have extremely wealthy donors, the disparity between a donor's and a staff member's financial status and social milieu can be difficult to navigate, and may feel uncomfortable at first. Development officers need to look the part, which can be difficult on a non-profit salary, and have to seamlessly move between roles. For example, at a black tie event, a development officer is both a guest and support staff, wearing a formal gown and chatting with donors and then later changing into jeans and sneakers to clean up after guests leave. Really, it means being able to connect to people on an essential level and not being fazed by the fact that a donor's car might cost more than a museum staffer's annual salary.
- Development directors in non-profits have an alarmingly high turnover rate. According to a 2013 study, 50 percent of development directors planned to leave their job within two years.[2] Various factors contribute to this high turnover, including, perhaps, executive directors' unrealistic expectations about the sums development professionals can raise. The silver lining here is high demand for development managers; however, prospective candidates should research this issue further. See chapter 15 for resources on the topic.

GRANT WRITER

In the interest of providing variety from the use of the term "manager," we'll use the term "writer" to talk about the person who oversees grants. However, the position entails more than the writing and will often be titled as a manager job. In micro, small, and mid-size museums, it's likely that one or more of the development managers will write grants as part of their regular duties, rather than having a dedicated grant writer.

In contrast to donations, which may be unsolicited, grants are gifts of money given by foundations (private and corporate) or government agencies on the municipal, state, or federal level. Grants require an application process and are often quite competitive. Grants range enormously in dollar amount, from several hundred dollars on a very local level to hundreds of thousands of dollars on the federal level. The complexity of the application usually correlates with the size of the grant award. A small grant from a town's cultural council, for example, may require only a letter explaining the project and how the funds will be used. A grant application for a federal agency like the National Endowment for the Humanities, the National Endowment for the Arts, or the Institute of Museum and Library Services may have several stages of review and require months—and a team of experts—to complete.

One of the main responsibilities of the grant writer is to research grant opportunities and determine first if the museum meets the eligibility requirements, and second, if the museum has a project or initiative that is a good fit for the grant. This is similar to the development manager's prospect researching. The research aspect of applying for grants is important to ensure that the museum is not wasting its resources: it takes time and money (the grant writer's salary, for instance) to apply for grants, so museums should only apply for those that are a good fit. Research also supports the museum's credibility, whereas a lack of research undermines it. If a museum applies for a grant without doing adequate legwork, the application may be misaligned with the grantor's goals or requirements. Submitting an application that is not well thought out can jeopardize the museum's chance of being successful with the same grantor at a different time, when a project *is* more appropriate.

Once the grant writer has identified appropriate grants, the next step is to consider the timeline. The larger the grant, the longer the lead time between the application's due date and the time when the funds will be provided to the successful applicant and can be spent on the funded project. A small grant may have a few cycles per year, with the funds available almost immediately, whereas a large federal grant will have to be planned well in advance; costs often cannot be incurred against the grant until the following year. The grant writer needs to determine, then, how the grant cycles line up with fundable projects. For example, if the museum applies for a grant to fund an exhibition, the lead time required for the grant has to correlate with the time frame for planning the exhibition.

In some cases, granting agencies encourage or even require a meeting with museum staff to help determine if an application is appropriate, to save time for both parties if it is not. If such a meeting isn't initiated by the granting agency, the grant writer can often request one, which the director and the manager of the particular project, such as the curator of an exhibition, may also attend.

Grant applications typically require gathering information about the museum and the project, creating a budget, and writing answers—known as the grant narrative—to the open-ended questions on the application. The amount of information that must be gathered depends on the grant. Basic requests include the museum's mission statement, list of board members, lists of past projects, and letters of support from outside organizations that will collaborate on the project. Organizing these documents requires good planning, as the grant writer must gather them from a variety of internal and external sources.

Grant budgets require detailed information about the cost of the project and how the grant award would be used. The costs are typically broken down into "hard" costs, or items the museum plans to pay for out of the grant award, and "soft" costs, or costs that are covered elsewhere in the museum's budget. Examples of hard costs include things like supplies, honoraria for experts hired to give lectures or teach a class, and travel. Soft costs include staff time and overhead (the costs associated with running the museum, such as utilities) and are usually calculated by percentage. For example, if an educator will be working on the project for ten hours of her forty-hour workweek, 25 percent of her salary can be put into the budget as a "soft cost." Input from staff involved in the project is vital to ensuring the budget's accuracy.

Many grants have a matching requirement. That means that if the grant application requests ten thousand dollars, the museum must put ten thousand dollars of its own funds toward the project. Soft and hard costs can both be counted toward the museum's match, but soft costs (particularly staff time) often make up the majority of the museum's match.

Once the grant writer has selected the grant and compiled the required information, the next step is to complete the narrative. This process requires the collaboration of the person who manages the project and can best explain its planning, implementation, and anticipated results. The grant writer must be sure to answer the questions that the grant asks rather than simply stating what the museum wants to convey about the project. The more specific an answer can be, the better. Most grant applications have word or page limits, so the grant writer has to be good at concisely conveying only the essential information.

Grant applications are most successful when they're authentic: when there is a demonstrated need and when the museum has carefully thought about how it will use the funds. I've seen instances where projects were created with the sole intent of attracting grants and other situations where the project was not well developed, resulting in a vague narrative that didn't answer the questions asked. Reviewers have enough experience to know when a request is not authentic or has been hastily put together. Grant writers have to mitigate against this and may have to explain to colleagues who are eager for funding why these tactics don't work.

Increasingly, granting agencies focus on outcomes and impact: how will the museum, and therefore the foundation or agency, know if the project has been successful, and whether the funds have been used to make a difference in the museum or the community. If assessment and outcomes are not already part of the project planning process, the grant writer needs to ensure that they are considered from the earliest conversations.

If a museum receives a grant, the funding usually has reporting requirements, meaning that the museum must demonstrate to the grantor how the funds were used and what impact the funding had. Most reports are due at the end of the grant cycle—often one year—but some require interim reports throughout the funding period. Because grant applications are written for future projects, changes often occur during the project implementation. Grantors accept the fact that not all aspects of a project can be anticipated and they usually allow for some amount of adjustment from the original plan. If the changes are significant, the grant writer will need to update the grantor and, sometimes, seek official approval for the grant funds to be used in a different way than initially planned.

A job as a grant writer may be a good fit for a person who:

- Is skilled at researching
- Writes well, of course, but especially is able to write prose that is clear, concise, and to the point, and that can explain museum initiatives in a way that is compelling and understandable to non-expert audiences. The grant reviewers will have expertise in their fields, but will not necessarily have a context for the proposed exhibition or project.
- Is adept at budgeting
- Works well under pressure
- Enjoys collaborating with colleagues
- Is organized and can work simultaneously on multiple projects with different timelines (say, write an application for a new grant and also write a report for a grant received last year)

Skills and experience that may help a candidate get hired as a grant writer:

- Business writing experience
- Project management
- Budgeting and forecasting
- Experience at a foundation or a corporation that awards grants; understanding the other side of the review process gives grant writers an advantage
- At least a BA, with a certificate or advanced degree often preferred

Keep in mind:

- Grant writing is inherently deadline driven.
- Grant writing jobs tend to be fairly senior; entry-level staff interested in grants are likely to start in another area of development.
- Nearly every staff member at a museum will be involved with a grant at some point, either by providing information for the application or report or through their work on a grant-funded project. Grant writing is a highly marketable skill for people interested in a wide range of museum departments (curatorial and education in particular) and is useful throughout the non-profit sector.
- Dedicated grant writer positions may be part-time. Many grant writers also work on a freelance basis.
- Occasionally, museums may propose compensating grant writers on a contingency basis, meaning they get paid a percentage of successful grant awards. Grant writers should avoid museums that follow this unethical practice.[3]

PROFILE

Jeanette O'Bryant, Development Officer, National Civil Rights Museum, Memphis, Tennessee

Jeanette O'Bryant
Courtesy of Jeanette O'Bryant

Jeanette describes her job as "working daily to create opportunities for cultivation and engagement with the donors of the National Civil Rights Museum." She continues, "I also oversee the membership program, work with the Director of Development on our major fundraising events, and manage our day-to-day fund development opportunities."

Though she had no prior museum experience before arriving at her current job, Jeanette had a previous contractual position in a non-profit. However, one relevant aspect of her background goes back to her childhood:

My church had a mission outreach program which included feeding and providing for those in need and a ministry with the women's prison in Parchman, Mississippi. At Christmas we delivered food and gifts to the families we served. As a child, I thought my own family did not have enough, and realizing that there were some who had nothing really helped me see that my community was bigger than me. The joy I felt being able to help someone ignited within me a desire to bring hope to someone in need.

Jeanette goes on to describe her favorite and least favorite parts of her job:

My favorite part of my job is meeting people. I love to hear our donors' stories about why they support the museum. My least favorite part is that, with a small staff, there is always so much work to do and not enough time or people to do it. This challenge also became a great takeaway: being stretched in many areas helps you enhance your existing skills and develop new ones. You often find a gift or talent you did not know you had.

Jeanette gives examples of some of the people she has encountered in her work:

I have met some amazing people at the museum, like Harry Belafonte, Ruby Dee, Myrlie Evers-Williams, and the 14th Dalai Lama. I had the opportunity to hear Rev. Jesse Jackson talk about his great memories at the Lorraine Motel prior to April 4, 1968 (the day Dr. Martin Luther King Jr. was assassinated while standing on the balcony of the motel, which is now part of the museum). Two weeks later, I heard Carolyn Champion, who lived at the Lorraine Motel with her parents, owners Walter and Loree Bailey, telling her story of how she remembered the same place, but as a resident. Moments like these fuel me for the work I do as a Development Officer. Some places are golden treasure boxes full of amazing things, memories, and connections. The National Civil Rights Museum is truly one of those places.

10

The Executive Office

EXECUTIVE DIRECTOR

A museum director provides leadership for the institution, motivates the board and the staff to be effective, and galvanizes support for the museum in myriad ways, such as attracting donations, expanding the collection, raising its profile, and positioning it as an integral part of its community. Though it may not always be advisable or realistic, one of the primary metrics on which a board evaluates the director is growth: how the museum has expanded, either literally or figuratively; and how it has increased its audience, built new partnerships, attracted new funding, secured more grants, enjoyed more press coverage, hosted more exhibitions, and so on. Being a director is an intense job; the expectations are high, and while a supportive board might encourage some experimentation, ultimately there is little room for failure.

As recently as a generation ago, a typical museum director would enjoy a long tenure—twenty, thirty, or more years—at one institution. Now, as in the rest of the workforce, such long periods at one museum are rare. A director is more likely to lead more than one museum in her career. Very frequently, a director starts at a micro or small museum, and when she moves on from a position, it's usually to a bigger institution. Directors tend to stay in one subset of museums—art museums, history museums, or university museums, for example—throughout their careers.

In chapter 2, in the discussion about organizational structure, we touched on the director's role and how it varies based on museum type. Here, we'll look in more detail about three areas of the director's job: working with the board, fundraising, and management. The director is the chief executive officer of the museum. The size of the institution dictates the extent to which the director participates in a hands-on manner in the day-to-day operation of the museum. In a micro or small museum, the director will perform vastly different types of tasks in a single day, such as shoveling snow from the front entrance of the museum, having lunch with a donor, and giving a tour to visitors. At mid-size and up, the director probably delegates most operational oversight to a deputy or associate director. In a large to jumbo museum, multiple associate directors, often called vice presidents or division heads, will each oversee a different arm of the museum's operations, such as education, curatorial, or development.

Generalizing about directors is difficult, because, more than any other job in the museum, the specifics depend on the individual, and not only on the institution, but on the stage of the museum's evolution. A director who is brought in to lead a capital campaign will not necessarily be the best person to steward the newly expanded museum a few years later; though the museum may be fundamentally the same, it requires different skills at different points in its trajectory. As is the case with a chief executive officer of any large corporation, a directorship takes shape depending on the individual's personality, background, skills, and interests. Directors don't wrap up their jobs at the end of the day; they veritably *inhabit* their jobs. The role is all-encompassing, even if the individual director remains diligent about carving out time for family, friends, and self-care. A director who is in charge of a museum that's a perfect fit for them can completely transform the institution, making it stronger. A good director always remembers the importance of putting the museum first, prioritizing what's best for the institution with every decision. If the museum's personality, so to speak, is inseparable from the director's, the museum runs the risk of being destabilized when that individual moves on.

Working with the Board

The board hires and supervises the director; a positive relationship with the board is key to the director's success. The board has responsibility for the governance of the museum and for its financial stability. Board committees (small groups of board members, often with outside participants or advisors) provide governance in specific areas: for example, the finance committee oversees the museum's budget and investments, and the collections committee votes on objects presented for acquisition or deaccession. In order to do their job effectively, board members rely on the director to provide relevant information. The director does this through regular communication and reports to the board; board meetings are one of the main vehicles for this communication. The frequency of these meetings varies; the law requires that all non-profits have at least one annual meeting. Many boards meet quarterly or bi-monthly; some may meet monthly. The director is an *ex officio* member of the board and of many of its committees but does not necessarily have to attend every committee meeting.[1]

A savvy director knows how to communicate with the board, both with individual trustees (though individuals cannot act alone in board business) and with the body as a whole. The director needs to be positive and have a "can-do" attitude with the board, while being realistic about challenges and optimistic about opportunities. This requires knowing each board member's skills and interests, and helping to channel that person's energy in the way that is most effective for the museum and most rewarding for the trustee.

One key point about working with the board is that there should be a clear division between the board's governance responsibilities and the director's management responsibilities.[2] For example, the board hires the director, but the director hires all other staff (at a mid-size or larger museum, the director may only hire senior staff, who in turn hire junior staff). The director may invite board members to sit on interview committees, but ultimately the director has the final say. A director needs to know when to call upon board members' expertise while also maintaining the delineation between his responsibilities and the board's.

With the input of the staff and invited members of the community, the director and the board work together to draft and approve the strategic plan, often with the help of an outside professional who brings objectivity.[3] The strategic plan outlines the museum's main goals—generally around five in number—for the upcoming three- to five-year period. The plan also includes initiatives and steps that will help the museum meet those goals, along with metrics for benchmarking. This plan is the tool that drives the day-to-day work of the museum and serves as the rubric against which the director's performance is measured.

In other types of museums—those that are not private non-profits—the reporting structure will vary. In college and university museums, the director might report to a dean or provost; in a municipal museum, the director might be supervised by the mayor or city manager; at a federal museum, the director reports to an administrator—for example, the directors of the presidential libraries report to the Archivist of the United States within the National Archives and Records Administration.[4]

Fundraising

In most private non-profit museums, one of the director's chief responsibilities is to raise funds for the institution. While the director often acts as the "face" of the museum in much of the fundraising, the board assists by making introductions to prospective donors, and the development office provides research and strategy, as discussed in chapter 9. The director engages in many different types of fundraising: soliciting donations through letters and appeals, hosting formal and informal meetings with potential donors, attending events in the community, and hosting fundraising events at the museum. In addition to formal fundraising initiatives, a savvy director spends a significant amount of time networking with individuals and representatives of organizations to learn more about them and to strategize about how to galvanize their support. Good directors work tirelessly to promote the museum and know that the most effective way to do so is through personal connections.

The director also supports the fundraising activities of the board. Not only should board members contribute to the museum financially, but they should also introduce the director (and other senior staff, when appropriate) to influential friends, colleagues, and institutions with whom they have an existing relationship. For example, perhaps the museum has been hoping to connect with the charitable foundation of a local corporation, but has been waiting for the right opportunity to do so. A board member who works at that company might arrange for the head of the charitable foundation to visit the museum for a tour followed by lunch. Typically, that board member and the director would meet with the potential donor, possibly with other staff as well. An initial meeting would provide a chance for the director to talk about the museum's current and upcoming projects, its work in the community, recent accomplishments, or other items of interest. This meeting would not include an "ask" (request for funds), but would set the groundwork for one at a more appropriate time. After the meeting, the director would follow up with a note to the potential donor and would check in periodically about projects they may have discussed. This type of cultivation takes a significant amount of the director's time, but ultimately, if done well, results in financial support for the museum.

In some cases, fundraising is not a key part of a director's job: for example, if the museum is funded by a large endowment or is part of a university or government agency, fundraising may be deemphasized or even prohibited. While being able to focus time and energy elsewhere may be considered a luxury, directors in those situations need to keep their fundraising skills honed in other ways (by grant writing or working with a friends' organization that supports the museum financially), so that they can easily transition to another institution where fundraising is a major part of the job.

Management

The level at which a director will manage staff depends on the staff size. At a micro or very small museum, the director usually directly supervises the other staff. At a museum on the larger side of "small," or at a mid-size museum, there might be an additional layer of supervision: staff report to department or division heads, who, in turn, report to the director. In a large or jumbo museum, the director supervises a small team of executive staff, or what might be thought of as the director's "cabinet." The makeup of this group will depend on the museum, but may include the senior most staff in several of the following departments: education, curatorial, exhibits, visitor services, development, security, and facilities.

Regardless of the number of direct reports, the director will perform supervisory functions for them such as goal setting, regular progress meetings, and assessment. The director or one of the senior team will also hold regular all-staff meetings. This is one way that the director communicates updates from the board to the staff.

Other aspects of management include responsibilities like reviewing financial information, signing checks, and negotiating contracts with vendors. Directors are often involved in the community on committees, with the town or municipality where the museum resides, and in partnerships with other cultural organizations and universities. For these reasons, as well as the fundraising tasks discussed previously, the director spends a good deal of time away from the office, representing the museum beyond its campus.

An underappreciated but crucial skill for a director is the ability to create a positive employee culture. Museums are so focused on serving their communities that they too often forget the community inside their own walls: their employees. Unfortunately, many directors come to their roles without having received much training in how to build a thriving employee culture. There are many ways to do so, though, and the most effective method for each director will be one that is authentic to their style and values. The director should establish policies and standards (with the board's input and approval if necessary) for competitive pay based on the cost of living in the area and equitable pay for all employees. Additionally, benefits should be as robust as the museum can possibly afford; I believe that it's worth cutting costs in other areas to ensure that employees are supported in doing their best work—it's that work that makes the museum what it is. Some aspects of employee culture are free and include things like transparency, respect, recognition of achievements, commitment to growth, adherence to a reasonable work schedule (the boss sets the example here), and, above all, clear communication of the institution's values.

While the three categories of board relations, fundraising, and management comprise much of a director's role, there are countless other responsibilities that fall outside of these areas: for example, building partnerships in the community, considering acquisitions for the collection, speaking about the museum in the press, being active in the American Alliance of Museums and regional affiliates, and managing large renovation or building projects. It's impossible to list them all here. One way to think about the scope of the director's role is to consider all the other roles discussed in this book and reflect on the fact that the director is responsible, at varying levels of remove, for making sure that all of these functions are carried out by competent people at the highest possible level.

A job as a museum director may be a good fit for a person who:

- Is an inspiring and authentic leader
- Believes in and can persuasively articulate the mission of the museum
- Is effective at fundraising
- Enjoys managing staff
- Has excellent interpersonal skills
- Is goal-oriented and driven
- Can prioritize and manage a large number of projects simultaneously
- Is comfortable as the public "face" of the museum
- Remains disciplined about drawing boundaries between work and home life to guard against burnout and to set a good example for other staff

Skills and experience that may help a candidate get hired as a museum director:

- Extensive experience in non-profit management, with museum-specific experience preferred
- Board relations experience
- Track record of successful fundraising
- Excellent communicator, especially in person and in writing
- Public speaking experience
- Budgeting and forecasting skills
- An advanced degree (MA, MBA, or PhD)

Keep in mind:

- Director jobs are extremely competitive. First-time directors often work at micro or small museums or work their way up through senior staff ranks. Note that moving from senior staff to director probably means moving to a different organization, rather than being promoted from within.
- Because of the competition, a director job may require a long-distance move; a person who starts as the director of a small museum and graduates to increasingly larger ones will probably move several times during their career.
- The director is at the top of the museum's organiztional chart (under the board), but not everyone is cut out for the director lifestyle; remember that there are many ways to lead, and leadership is possible at every level.

DEPUTY DIRECTOR

A deputy director, sometimes called an associate director or the chief operating officer, is the second-in-command on a museum staff. Note that in a very large to jumbo museum, there may be more than one deputy director, such as a deputy director for external affairs or a deputy director for interpretation and programs. In these cases, one person may be designated as senior deputy director, or they may simply take turns stepping in to the director's role when the director is away.

The deputy director shares many of the director's responsibilities—budgeting, planning, supervising—but there are a few key differences: first, the deputy director reports to the director rather than to the board, and second, as a general rule, the deputy director is more inward-focused than outward-focused. As noted, the director spends quite a bit of time out of the office, focusing on the board, meeting with donors, and representing the museum in the community. Therefore, the deputy director handles much of the day-to-day work of the museum, managing staff, running meetings, troubleshooting when issues come up, and so forth. The deputy director usually attends board meetings and some committee meetings as an invited guest, though not necessarily in an *ex officio* capacity.

The deputy director acts as a liaison between the director and junior staff. The deputy director will bring staff issues and input to the director and in turn will convey policies and other information that affects the staff back to them. This role is especially important in a very large or jumbo museum, where junior staff rarely interact with the director.

Like the director, the deputy director also represents the museum in the community and with partners, because extending the reach of the museum outside of its walls is so important.

A job as a deputy director may be a good fit for a person who:

- Might aspire to be a museum director
- Enjoys supervising staff
- Can manage many responsibilities simultaneously
- Believes in and can promote the mission of the museum
- Is skilled at managing all aspects of museum operations
- Enjoys working with a wide variety of people, from visitors to board members
- Is comfortable stepping in to the director's role when the director is away

Skills and experience that might help a candidate get hired as a deputy director:

- At least seven to ten years of museum or previous non-profit experience
- Strategic planning
- Project management
- Staff supervision
- Public speaking
- Excellent communication skills
- An MA or other advanced degree is usually required; the type of degree will depend on the specifics of the role and the museum

Keep in mind:

- Advancing from deputy director to director will probably involve moving to another museum; it's relatively rare for a deputy director to be promoted internally.
- Deputy directors have many of the same responsibilities as the director, but are usually paid significantly less. Another way to put it is that the deputy director experiences, say, only 25 percent less stress than the director, but probably receives at least 50 percent less pay.
- Though not quite as much of an around-the-clock job as the director's, the deputy director role requires a flexible schedule, including regular evenings and weekends.

EXECUTIVE ASSISTANT

In mid-size and larger museums, the executive assistant is a key member of the director's team. (In museums smaller than mid-size, the director may have an assistant who also works with other staff or performs other duties, rather than a dedicated assistant.) The executive assistant makes it possible for the director to do their job. The assistant manages the director's calendar, books travel, assists with correspondence, prepares documents, and otherwise makes sure that the director spends time on the big picture rather than on details that can be delegated.

The executive assistant serves as the first line of contact for both internal and external requests for the director's time. While this may sound straightforward, it's actually quite complex and requires that the executive assistant knows which requests to prioritize, which to decline, which to pass on to another staff member, and which require more information or follow-up. Because the director spends a huge amount of time in meetings, building the schedule is not unlike putting together a puzzle, making sure not only that the meetings are booked, but also that the director is prepared (with agendas, talking points, or other necessary material) and that follow-up happens in a timely manner after the meeting. Once that schedule is built, the executive assistant needs to make sure the director adheres to it as much as possible, so one meeting that runs late doesn't jeopardize the rest of the day. The importance of the executive assistant's role is underscored by the especially close working relationship they have with the director. The executive assistant is likely the only person on staff who is allowed—indeed, is expected—to interrupt meetings, cut conversations short, or do whatever is required to keep the director on schedule.

The executive assistant job is the one position in the museum where it's appropriate for an assistant to handle personal tasks for a supervisor (within reason, of course). As the director's job is all-consuming, the boundaries between work and home are fluid. For example, the executive assistant may plan the director's personal travel as well as business travel, or assist with logistics for a fundraising event taking place at the director's home. Because the executive assistant has a glimpse into the director's life outside of work, and because she also works with museum VIPs (board members, directors of other museums, elected officials), discretion and confidentiality are absolutely essential.

The executive assistant acts as a liaison between the director and other groups, notably the staff and the board. In terms of the staff, the executive assistant will arrange the director's attendance at meetings, will follow through on staff requests of the director (e.g., ensure that a document gets the director's signature), and will make requests of staff for things that the director needs (such as asking a curator for a few bullet points to add to remarks at an exhibition opening). Similarly, the executive assistant will facilitate communication between the board and the director. In some museums, that may include helping to prepare for and set up board meetings, compiling agendas and packages of information the board needs to review before the meeting.

A job as an executive assistant may be a good fit for a person who:

- Is always organized
- Effectively manages scheduling and maintains calendars
- Can politely and efficiently communicate with a wide variety of people via phone, online, and in person
- Feels comfortable acting as the director's gatekeeper, including saying no to requests when necessary
- Is unflappable—handles stress well and projects a calm and confident demeanor even in difficult or heated situations
- Believes that early is on time, on time is late, and late is unacceptable

Skills and experience that may help a candidate get hired as an executive assistant:

- Prior experience working with executives or other high-level professionals
- Scheduling
- Booking travel
- General office skills
- Writing experience (to help with the director's correspondence)
- Ability to act with discretion and to honor confidentiality
- An associate degree or a BA; recommendations also carry a lot of weight with this role

Keep in mind:

- This is one of those jobs where the people who are good at it are excellent, and the people who aren't good don't last very long. The role is crucial to making the director's office run smoothly, and the chemistry between the executive assistant and the director is key.
- Though occasionally the executive assistant may be asked to stay late or come in on a Saturday, it's usually understood that as an administrative job, the position enjoys a (mostly) regular schedule.
- While an executive assistant to the director has little—if any—room for promotion within the museum, this is a job that's easily transferable outside of the field, as most large non-profits, universities, and corporations have similar roles.
- This job likely requires professional dress every day, even on Mondays (the equivalent of casual Fridays in museums, when they're usually closed to the public).

PROFILE

Rebekah Beaulieu, Director, Florence Griswold Museum, Old Lyme, Connecticut

After entering the field with the goal of becoming a curator, Rebekah had the foresight to realize that diversifying her skills would make her a more competitive candidate for executive-level museum jobs down the road. She implemented that strategy by completing her PhD and working in nonprofit fundraising, both of which perfectly positioned her for her current role, which she has occupied since 2018.

Rebekah Beaulieu
Courtesy of Florence Griswold
Museum

My training was twofold: I prioritized concurrent trajectories in management and in scholarship. I originally started on the curatorial track and interned in education and curatorial departments in museums such as the Milwaukee Art Museum and the National Portrait Gallery, and received my first master's degree in art history and museum studies. I then reached a crossroads: I was based in the Midwest and there were simply not that many opportunities for a recent MA grad who wanted a curatorial position. I started thinking about what other areas of museum work would give me a leg up and decided to work in development. I worked in social services and the performing arts sector with a focus on individual giving. It was quite the pivot, I admit, but completely worth it.

As a director, Rebekah appreciates the support of her team: "My favorite part of my job is working with our team here at the Florence Griswold Museum, and I refer herein to our staff, our volunteers, and our trustees. It is an extremely capable, professional, and committed group of people that I honestly enjoy working alongside every day." Like most directors, Rebekah sees time as the most precious commodity: "My least favorite part is that I wish there were more hours in the day! Between meetings and events, the daily work, and the board and service work I do through professional organizations, there simply isn't enough time to do everything I love to do!"

She goes on to describe a "typical" day (though there is no such thing in a director's world):

I arrive as early as possible, usually before everyone else. This helps me get a jumpstart on the day while it is quiet in the office and it is usually the only part of the day I can fully control! After that, it is usually some balance of correspondence, emails or thank-you notes (I spend a *lot* of my day writing thank yous), phone calls and meetings with staff, and talking with people: trustees who stop by, school groups and guided tours, and members of the public.

Rebekah has two key pieces of advice for aspiring museum professionals:

First, every person who you may think has it made in museums has dealt with challenges. I had situations in my past where I faced frustrations and watched others move forward as I felt like I was sitting on the sidelines. Every single person's trajectory is different and you will encounter bumps in the road: do not be deterred when your path is not easy. Second, do not be afraid to dive in and learn about things that scare you. I would have never anticipated learning as much about management and finance as I have, but it has been invaluable to my career path.

11

Administration

In this chapter, we will discuss key support roles within the museum's administration. Unlike many of the jobs in previous chapters, these jobs are not museum-specific. That is, these positions are not exclusive to museums, but in the museum context they do have elements that distinguish them from similarly defined jobs elsewhere. Because the positions in this chapter are broadly applicable to other fields, what we'll focus on here are the aspects that *are* more museum-specific. People who are interested in these fields will want to do additional research about the universal aspects of these jobs.

In the preface, I wrote about many of the intangible benefits of working in museums, and those are worth re-examining here. The jobs in this chapter are, frankly, jobs that could be performed in for-profit companies for significantly more pay and better perks. So why, then, would someone choose to do these jobs at a museum? Simply put, the environment of a museum workplace—its energy and dynamism— is hard to resist. Where else can you take a break from your desk to walk through galleries to view world-class objects, engage in continual (usually free!) learning opportunities, or work with people who are committed to preserving and interpreting objects and engaging with the community?

Ask any museum employee what they like best about their job, and more often than not, they'll talk about the people they work with. Not only do their colleagues have fascinating jobs within the museum, but they also tend to have interesting lives outside of work—they are artists, reenactors, historians, they volunteer at other nonprofits, and otherwise are engaged in creative pursuits. Certainly these things can be true of the workforce at any company; companies committed to positive employee culture can probably compete with museums in terms of wonderful colleagues, but no other environment is quite like a museum.

Another reason to work at a non-profit is the sense of helping to create a more vibrant community and to provide people with educational resources and experiences. It's not only the director, educators, and curators who do this; everyone who works at a museum, even behind the scenes, contributes to the mission in some way. An exemplary museum workplace will help all employees see how they fit into the bigger, mission-driven picture.

Whether or not these reasons compel someone to seek out one of these roles at a museum instead of pursuing higher-paying opportunities elsewhere is a decision that depends on many factors related to the job market and the individual's personal or family situation. A museum position may be a good place to hone skills or learn new ones, or to get a taste of a non-profit institution, even if a job outside of the field may be the next step.

HUMAN RESOURCES MANAGER

The human resources (HR) manager handles all aspects of employee relations at the museum. From the moment employees are hired until the moment they leave the museum (voluntarily or involuntarily), the HR manager is one of their contacts. HR managers—or their junior staff members—work with employees both on an operational level (such as processing payroll or managing the annual review process) and on a policy level. A significant part of the job entails ensuring adherence with museum policy as well as with state and federal regulations that all employers must follow.

Very few small to mid-size museums have dedicated HR departments. In these cases, HR duties may be handled by the director, a finance manager or assistant (who may process payroll or track time off), or contracted out to an outside vendor. Large and jumbo museums do generally have HR managers and likely have additional staff in the department as well.

In setting policy, such as determining the rate at which employees accrue paid time off, drafting a dress code, or establishing compensation guides, the HR manager works closely with the director (or, in a jumbo museum, one of the deputy directors or vice presidents), and perhaps also with a committee of the board. The HR manager also oversees benefits packages, working with insurance companies and other vendors to get competitive rates, and helping employees access the benefits offered. An unfortunate reality is that a large part of the negotiations with insurance companies is devoted to keeping costs down and keeping plans affordable for employees in the face of ever-increasing rates.

Another important part of the HR manager's job is handling conflicts, like disputes between employees, disciplinary issues, or poor or inadequate performance. To do this well, she must be a clear communicator who practices fairness and compassion, while holding employees to high—but realistic—expectations.

The HR manager makes sure that appropriate documents are in place and updated regularly, such as job descriptions and employee files. She also ensures that the museum keeps current with best practices and relevant laws related to things like overtime, accommodations for disabilities, sexual harassment reporting, and whistleblower protections.

In a museum structure, people who assume management roles—meaning anyone who supervises other employees—often do not receive adequate training to do so. Many people simply work their way up the career ladder in their departments and eventually find themselves with people reporting to them. Of course there are exceptions, but it is far too often the rule that museum supervisors lack significant management training. Supervising employees is a specialized skill that must be practiced and honed, rather than expecting it to come naturally with seniority. Therefore, HR managers' jobs are crucial, because they may be the people who are not only ensuring adherence to policies and laws, but who are also explaining to other staff why those policies and laws are in place and how they must be implemented. Unfortunately, though, many museums, especially micro and small ones, see HR expertise as an optional, rather than necessary, cost.

As the field slowly but surely moves toward improving museum workplaces (more on this topic in chapter 13), I believe that the HR manager job will become increasingly important, and that more museums will realize that they need assistance from a professional in this area, whether full-time, part-time, or on a consulting basis. A job as an HR manager may be a good fit for a person who:

- Knows applicable employment laws on a state and federal level
- Is policy- and procedure-oriented
- Can act as a liaison between the institution and its employees
- Enjoys working with people and supporting them to perform well in their jobs
- Communicates clearly, confidently, and compassionately when dealing with difficult employee issues, and is able to put emotions aside

Skills and experience that may help a person get hired as an HR manager:

- Familiarity with payroll or benefits administration
- Communication skills, especially in negotiation or mediation
- Commitment to confidentiality
- Ability to stay up-to-date on changing laws and policies
- Experience establishing and writing policies such as an employee handbook or a dress code
- For some museums, experience negotiating with or managing union employees is a desirable skill.
- At least a BA, if not an MBA or management certificate

Keep in mind:

- While I hope this is changing, some museum professionals in supervisory roles, though they act with good intentions, do not uphold best practices in regard to HR; this results from museums being under-resourced and having too few accessible and affordable management training programs. Therefore, an HR manager coming into a museum may be entering a situation where significant work is required to get the museum to a basic level of compliance.
- In general, museum professionals are underpaid, and too few have reliable full-time jobs with health care and other essential benefits. An HR manager may find this situation frustrating and slow to change, making it difficult to retain good employees.

FACILITIES MANAGER

The facilities manager is the unsung hero of the museum world. Though the director and most of the staff know how crucial the role is, it is otherwise behind the scenes. The basic role of a facilities manager, along with subordinate staff, is to ensure that the building(s) and grounds of the museum, and all of their systems, are operating efficiently and serving the needs of the institution. The scope of the position includes overseeing maintenance work, such as janitorial services, landscaping, and snow removal. The job also entails supervising contractors, keeping current with inspections and code updates, and managing systems inside and outside the building. The major system that a facilities manager in a museum worries about (and probably—justifiably—complains about) is the heating, venting, and air-conditioning (HVAC) system. Because most museums have some level of climate control in order to maintain a safe environment for the objects, this system is the most important in the building, much more so than in other types of settings.

The HVAC system needs to maintain certain levels of temperature and humidity in the galleries or spaces that house objects; the levels may differ throughout the building depending on the types of materials in the collection. Because these demands are more stringent than other applications for the same systems, problems can arise. In a museum setting, those problems may be urgent: if the temperature or humidity suddenly fluctuates dramatically, the safety of the collection may be at risk.

As in all the jobs we've discussed, the particulars of this role depend to a large extent on the size of the museum. At a micro or small museum, the facilities manager often does most of the hands-on work himself, though he may contract out some things, like cleaning, landscaping, or snow plowing. As a jack-of-all-trades, the facilities manager does a combination of smaller tasks (repairs, painting, moving or setting up furniture, monitoring thermostats, changing lightbulbs) and larger tasks, such as gathering bids and selecting contractors for large repairs. There may be some responsibilities that, in a larger museum, would not fall under the facilities department. For example, if there is not a separate security staff, the facilities manager in a micro or small museum might be the point person for the alarm system. In a mid-size or larger museum, the facilities manager has several staff members for the smaller, more maintenance-oriented tasks, allowing him the time to oversee larger projects and initiatives.

Good facilities managers are indispensable, giving them some measure of job security. Institutional knowledge about the building(s) and grounds—and their idiosyncrasies—is hard to replace.

A job as a facilities manager may be a good fit for a person who:

- Wants a very active, hands-on job with lots of variety
- Enjoys problem solving
- Understands a wide variety of mechanical systems
- Appreciates the uniqueness of a museum setting from a facilities point of view (e.g., the fact that it has climate control requirements that probably differ from most other types of buildings)
- Likes both working alone and working as a tcam
- Doesn't mind engaging with the public, though this is not the primary function of his job

Skills and experience that may help a candidate get hired as a facilities manager:

- Experience in one or more of the many hands-on tasks the manager might take on, like carpentry, maintenance work, landscaping, or painting
- Working with vendors, including getting quotes, negotiating contracts, and overseeing the work
- Understanding of requirements for complying with the Americans with Disabilities Act
- HVAC knowledge and experience is especially valuable
- Supervisory experience
- Computer skills—both general office skills (email, calendars) and skills related to computerized monitoring of mechanical systems
- A BA is likely not required, though it may be helpful, as may other types of certification or licenses

Keep in mind:

- Being a facilities manager absolutely requires a flexible schedule, not only to respond to emergencies, but also, perhaps, to attend some events (say, to help with setup and cleanup). Facilities managers should expect to at least occasionally get calls in the middle of the night and to check on the museum during storms. For these reasons, the facilities manager may find it beneficial to live close to the museum rather than having to face a long commute during those urgent situations.

- Though the work is hands-on, facilities managers deal with nearly every employee in the museum and may also interact with visitors—say, explaining to visitors that a space is temporarily closed for cleaning, or assisting someone with the wheelchair lift. People skills are, therefore, equally important.
- This is a very physical job, which may be a concern if the manager gets injured or finds some tasks harder to complete as he gets older; this is especially the case if he works alone, and less of an issue if he supervises a team.
- Though the role is incredibly important to a well-functioning museum, it may not be perceived that way by those who think that an employee's value corresponds to his or her place on the organizational chart.
- In some museums, the facilities manager position may be part-time and/or hourly, without benefits.

DIRECTOR OF FINANCE

The director of finance oversees everything having to do with the inflow and outflow of funds to the museum. This includes managing the museum's accounts (checking, savings, investments), creating and tracking budgets, preparing checks, paying invoices, and managing cash. The director of finance follows Generally Accepted Accounting Procedures, or GAAP, which outlines best practices, policies, procedures, and legal responsibilities related to managing an organization's money.[1] Note that accounting in a non-profit organization differs in some ways from accounting in a for-profit business. The main distinction is that a non-profit is mission-driven, providing a benefit to society rather than existing primarily to make money. Therefore, some of the reporting and types of statements required by non-profits reflect that difference. Another distinction is that museums often have restricted funds whose use must be tracked. These are funds that can only be applied toward certain expenses; for example, a donor may designate how funds may be used, grant money is usually earmarked for a specific use, or funds may be raised for a particular purpose, like a building project.

A finance director should also enforce internal controls—these are checks and balances within the organization to ensure that errors are caught quickly and that no funds are being mishandled. Perhaps the most important internal control is segregation of duties, meaning that no one person has total control over any aspect of the finances. For example, the finance director usually prepares the checks but does not have check signing privileges (these are usually reserved for the director and one or more board members); allowing one staff member to have both of these duties could increase the museum's risk for fraud.

Though finance managers do not physically carry out all of the tasks related to money management, they train and oversee the people who do. This includes anyone in the museum who processes incoming payments of any kind, such as staff at the front desk, the shop or café, the programs office, and the development office. Cash, credit cards, checks, and online payments must all be tracked, recorded, and reconciled to be sure they match. Any discrepancies must be identified and explained.

Careful tracking also takes place on the expense side, to make sure that all purchases made by staff, through credit cards, petty cash, checks, purchase orders, or online transfers are approved and tracked to the correct department, and that shipments of goods match their invoices. The finance director also manages records for all museum vendors, making sure the museum receives and pays invoices on an appropriate schedule.

The finance director (or a junior staff member) has regular tasks related to reconciling accounts, reporting numbers, and comparing the actual numbers to the budget. Some of these are daily, weekly, or bi-weekly (such as reconciling the cash deposits or running payroll); some are monthly (reconciling the bank statement and the credit card bill); others coincide with board meetings; and some are annual, like compiling figures for the annual report.

The finance director works closely with the director and senior staff to define and track departmental budgets, and also works with the finance committee of the board, which is ultimately responsible for passing each year's proposed budget. If a museum has an independent audit (which may be required or may be voluntary), the finance director will work with the outside auditors to make sure they have all the documents they require to perform the audit.

At a micro or small museum, many accounting functions may be outsourced. For example, the museum may hire an outside accountant or bookkeeper or may hire a professional to help with tax returns.

A job as a finance director may be a good fit for a person who:

- Excels at math and accounting-related skills, including financial analysis
- Understands and knows how to follow GAAP
- Is a meticulous recordkeeper
- Enjoys working with staff across the museum and with the board
- Can skillfully communicate financial information to colleagues who don't have financial backgrounds
- Has a creative approach to cutting expenses and increasing revenue

Skills and experience that might help a candidate get hired as a finance director:

- Bookkeeping or banking experience
- Budgeting and forecasting
- Cash handling
- Payroll experience
- Computer skills, especially spreadsheet and accounting software
- At least a BA; a Certified Public Accountant (CPA) license may be preferred

Keep in mind:

- Finance staff in museums usually enjoy a fairly regular schedule, though there may be a time crunch around the end of the fiscal year.
- In museums with small or especially tight budgets, finance directors have to prioritize expenses, find ways to increase income, and, sometimes, assist the director with some very difficult decisions, like cutting staff positions.
- This job is highly transferable in general, though staff moving between sectors need to understand the differences between non-profit and corporate accounting.

INFORMATION TECHNOLOGY SPECIALIST

In a museum setting, the information technology (IT) team may work in multiple realms: the offices, where they manage the computer systems that staff use; online, where they oversee the museum's website; and the public spaces of the museum, where they manage technology that visitors use as part of their experience. This visitor-oriented realm could include things like iPads in the galleries or technology-based interactives. In a museum that exhibits and/or collects contemporary art, the IT specialist may be involved in installing, maintaining, and troubleshooting works of art or installations that use technology. The IT specialist may also work with audiovisual systems, though large and jumbo museums may have a separate audiovisual department.

To support staff's use of technology, the IT specialist selects, purchases, installs, maintains, and services the hardware and software throughout the building. Depending on the museum, there may be several systems operating in different parts of the building: a point-of-sale system at the front desk, shop, and café; a collections management database in the curatorial department; a constituent management database in the development department; enrollment or student management software if the museum has a large studio art school or other similar program; and box office or ticketing software if the museum has a film series or other programming that reaches a large audience. All of these systems require expertise to keep them—and all of the museum's operations—running smoothly.

The museum's website—more than ever a crucial part of the museum's outreach to the public—may be housed in one of several departments, depending on the size of the museum and the website's complexity. Some large to jumbo museums have an entire web team; smaller museums may situate the website in the marketing/graphic design realm. Multiple staff people may have permission to update portions of the website that correspond to the areas they oversee: for example, the education team may post programs on a calendar; the shop manager may oversee the e-commerce function, if the website includes one; the café manager might post seasonal menus. Although there may be many hands involved in keeping the website updated and ensuring that it's graphically pleasing and user-friendly, the IT specialist will have some responsibility for maintaining the back end of the website.

A job as an IT specialist may be a good fit for a person who:

- Wants to use their IT skills in a stimulating cultural environment
- Can work well under pressure if there is a problem, but can also deal with regular maintenance issues
- Can provide support and explain issues to staff who do not have IT expertise
- Knows, or can quickly learn, specialized museum software
- Enjoys working with artists who use technology in their art (a possibility in contemporary art museums)

Skills and experience that may help a candidate get hired as an IT specialist:

- Prior experience in an area related to IT, such as computer repair
- Experience selecting and purchasing equipment, training staff, and migrating data to new software
- Experience with the types of software used in museums (knowledge of specific products the museum uses may be a plus), such as databases for development or the collection, e-commerce, and point of sale systems
- Web design and/or maintenance experience
- Customer service experience
- Problem solving
- Ability to work well under pressure
- Some background in the content area of the museum (history, art, etc.) may be a plus, though likely not required
- A BA, an associate's degree, or—given the myriad ways people find their way into IT —equivalent experience; an advanced degree or certificate may be preferred, especially at large and jumbo museums

Keep in mind:

- Only large to jumbo museums are likely to have a full-time IT staff of one or more people. In other museums, IT will be part of another job. In micro or small museums, IT is likely to be outsourced.
- Limited budgets may make it difficult for museums to keep up with hardware and software purchases, meaning that IT staff will be maintaining older systems, which can be frustrating.
- It's an understatement to say that people with IT expertise could make higher salaries in the for-profit sector. However, there are lifestyle benefits to working in a museum (or non-profit) rather than a corporation. For example, the job is likely to have regular hours and only rarely require weekends. Plus, as noted at the beginning of the chapter, museums are compelling places to work. That can be a tough sell, though, for IT specialists who are repaying student loans or living in an expensive area.

PROFILE

Douglas Perkins, Associate Director, Operations and Finance, Middlebury College
Museum of Art, Middlebury, Vermont

Douglas Perkins
Courtesy of Douglas Perkins

Doug has a multifaceted job that includes many of the functions discussed in this chapter, as well as several covered in previous chapters. His insight about working at a college museum makes his comments especially useful to readers who are potentially interested in an academic museum setting. Doug distills his job down to this short description: "I oversee all aspects of the day-to-day operation of the museum. Most notably, I manage all of the museum's budgeting and accounting functions, endowments, communications, digital engagement, grants and contracts, donor relations, and human resources." He has a broad background encompassing different fields, including one that might seem irrelevant but actually provides valuable experience; the combination prepared him well for his job:

A bachelor's degree in economics—training in the principles of accounting and corporate finance—has proven helpful in navigating the financial side of operating a museum. A minor in art history has equipped me to engage with visitors and to communicate the essence of what we collect and exhibit. But what I find most useful are the intangibles that a liberal arts education confers: creative thinking, problem solving, time and resource management, relationship and capacity building, and the habituation of ongoing personal development. My position is impossibly broad and diverse, and success requires a similarly broad and diverse set of skills. I should also give a nod to five years of bartending, which taught me how to multitask like a boss.

One of the best things about a job like Doug's is the breadth of experience it provides, some of which are listed in the job description, and some of which fall under "other duties as assigned." Doug explains:

While larger museums can afford to hire people for very specific jobs—graphic designer, web developer, social media manager, preparator, HR manager, etc.—smaller museums, and academic museums in particular, rely on personnel who can wear many hats and wear them well. I handle everything from international bank transfers and currency exchange to graphic design to front end web development to grant writing to fax and copier repair, sometimes all in the same day. It's not uncommon to walk past a gallery and get roped into helping to install a painting.

Academic museums have some clear pros and cons. Doug cites "working with students" as the best part and "navigating the politics of academia" as his least favorite. No two days at an academic museum—or any museum, really—are alike. Doug lists some highlights that took place over a recent series of days:

> I designed a suite of advertisements and posters for an upcoming exhibit; coded a couple of web forms; converted a contract payment into Guatemalan quetzals and figured out how to get it delivered to a guy in the middle of the Guatemalan jungle; bid successfully at auction for a painting by a little-known mid-seventeenth-century woman artist; performed an exorcism on a colleague's heavily malwared laptop; edited and submitted an IMLS grant application; had a Twitter convo with Cheech Marin about contemporary Latinx art in his collection; and boosted a Facebook post for a tattoo exhibit that went viral.

Doug has three pieces of advice that apply to any museum job, in any department or setting:

> First, develop some serious project management skills and become familiar with several of the more popular project management platforms. You may not know in advance which platform a particular museum may be using, but if you can show with confidence that you can step into any platform and lead the way, then you'll have a leg up. 2) Learn how to multi-task and be ready to highlight moments when you've juggled an entire troop of snarling, rabid monkeys without breaking a sweat. 3) Learn how to learn: in other words, become a master of knowing how to find answers and acquire missing skill sets in real time.

My favorite insight from Doug is his description of why he remains committed to the field, despite the occasional frustration. While his comments apply to his work at an art museum, similar statements could be made for any type of museum that illuminates a subject through mission-driven, visitor-centered work. He says,

> Art has many powers, but in particular it has the power to heal and to bring people together. As the global population mushrooms and more people try to find their places on this planet we will naturally feel less connected. Art can counteract that trend, and every day when I step into my office I have an opportunity to help lead visitors to find their own connections to art objects and to other people through those objects. Art communicates the hopes, dreams, anxieties, and imperatives of humanity in ways that other forms of expression cannot, and museum workers provide the public with access to that in myriad ways. It's an enormously important role that we fill in our society.

12

Universal Skills and Distinct Pathways

In the last several chapters, this book has outlined skills and experience that may be required for specific jobs. Many of these overlap between jobs, and, given the complexity of museum jobs, and the variance from one institution to the next, many skills were inevitably left out of the lists. In this chapter, I will discuss what we might call global skills. These are talents that may not be specifically required for every museum job, but they are talents that can only benefit people who have them. Not only do they have the ability to give candidates the edge in a very competitive field, but because they're universal, they also make it easier for museum employees to be flexible within the museum. This flexibility could be crucial in the case of layoffs or if moving up the ladder means becoming responsible for part of the museum outside the employee's immediate area of expertise. Arguably, these skills would benefit a job candidate in any field; they're universal beyond our parameters here. They're particularly valuable in museums, I believe, which I'll discuss more throughout this chapter. I'll also provide a few ideas about how readers can build skills in these areas outside of (or in addition to) academic training.

COMMUNICATION: WRITING

Writing and public speaking are two communication skills that are crucial to some museum roles but are helpful to nearly all. First, let's look at writing. Virtually all of the content that museums share with their constituents—visitors, members, volunteers—starts as a written document. Here, I'm referring not only to texts whose final form is print—labels, exhibition signage, gallery guides, brochures, newsletters, appeal letters, membership materials, lesson plans, among many others—but also content that is delivered in other ways. Every calendar listing, audio tour script, interpreter training manual, lecture, and speech was, at one point, a written document.

The writing that museum staff do on a daily basis falls into two main categories: expository and persuasive. Expository writing is the type of writing practiced by curators, educators, archivists, and other staff who write to provide information to visitors (or other audiences, such as website users). This writing builds on content research as well as on knowledge of the audience. It's engaging but clear; it doesn't use jargon; it makes connections to visitors' personal experiences; it makes complex ideas accessible; it probes difficult or controversial topics to uncover their main points of debate. Excellent expository writing requires practice; academic writing can be a good foundation, but, for the most part, museum writing is not the same as academic writing, which often seems dense and jargony to non-specialists. (One exception may be at university and college museums; given their audiences, academic language is appropriate.)

The other type of writing practiced in museums is persuasive writing. I'm not referring to the type of persuasive writing many of us learned in high school, in which the writer picks a side of an issue and tries to convince the reader to agree. Nor am I referring to gimmicky sales writing. Museums use persuasive writing in a number of ways. Development materials, like letters, invitations, membership collateral, and thank-you letters make a case for why the museum needs financial (and other) support and provide compelling evidence for how the funds make a difference. Press releases and marketing materials aim to convince the press and the public to visit the museum to see a particular exhibition or attend a particular event. Many of the characteristics of expository writing also apply to persuasive writing, such as clarity and helping readers connect to the text. Persuasive writing differs in its goal, which is to garner the support, in one way or another, of the reader.

Skill Building in Writing

Write, write, write. Simply put, writing is a skill that must be practiced and practiced often. Grades and comments on college papers are one way to assess current writing skill. Students who are not excelling in this area should take full advantage of their school's writing center, which provides free tutoring and writing help. For readers who are not current students, find other ways to practice: go back to an old academic paper and rewrite sections that an instructor flagged as problematic or write letters to the editor, blog posts, book reviews on Amazon, or a letter to send along with holiday cards. People with an inclination toward creative writing should by all means continue to practice that art form, but should also consider ways to practice the type of writing that might be useful in a museum setting.

COMMUNICATION: PUBLIC SPEAKING

Many museum staff have an explicit need for public speaking skills in their day-to-day work: curators give lectures and gallery talks, educators teach workshops and lead tours, development staff address groups of donors, public relations staff speak to the press, and so on. In many other positions, the need for public speaking skills is less apparent or may even seem remote. Perhaps the most common reason for "behind the scenes" staff to find themselves addressing a group is at a micro or small museum where the phrase "all hands on deck" is a frequent mantra. For example, on a day when an interpreter calls in sick just before a large school group arrives at the museum, any available staff member might have to pinch-hit. As another example, museum staff might be invited to participate in career day at the local school. The press might be interested in speaking to not just the curator of an exhibition, but also to the preparator who installed an especially complicated object. Or consider the extensive interviews with security staff about the 1990 theft from the Isabella Stewart Gardner Museum on the *Last Seen* podcast co-produced by the Boston *Globe* and WBUR, Boston's National Public Radio affiliate; admittedly this is an extraordinary example, but it underscores the point that any staff member could, at some point, be required to speak in public.

Skill Building in Public Speaking

Public speaking comes easier for some people than others, but everyone can improve their skill in this area by taking a course (in person or online) or finding a coach. Toastmasters is a non-profit organization that focuses on providing public speaking opportunities for its members; there are chapters throughout the country and around the world. Like writing, public speaking is a skill that gets easier the more it's practiced. Everyone can find opportunities to try it out: speaking up at a meeting, asking a question at a lecture, reading to a local classroom, or video recording themselves speaking and then watching it with a critical eye (painful, I know, but useful).

CUSTOMER SERVICE

Like writing and public speaking, customer service is a skill that may not be required for many museum jobs but that is always useful. In essence, everyone who works at a museum is there to support the visitor experience in some way. Visitor services, membership, security, education, shop staff, and café staff are some of the main practitioners of customer service, but in a visitor-focused museum, all staff should be expected to go out of their way to help visitors. A common scenario is the "all hands on deck" example outlined previously: especially in a micro or small museum, any staff member may be called upon to answer the phones or process admissions if the museum is short-staffed or if visitor services needs help on a particularly busy day. While that may not be a likely scenario in a mid-size or larger museum, visitors encounter staff from nearly all departments in the public spaces of the museum: the exhibitions team installing an exhibition, the development staff setting up an event, or any staff member taking advantage of the shop's employee discount or sharing the elevator with visitors. In all these situations, and countless similar ones, the staff person should be able to answer questions, give directions, or simply smile and ask if the visitors are enjoying their time at the museum. To go a step further, staff should anticipate questions rather than wait for them: if visitors in the elevator are wondering aloud where to meet for the eleven o'clock tour, a staff member who overhears them should chime in and help them out.

Skill Building in Customer Service

Anyone who has worked in retail, food service, or in the tourism or hospitality industries will have some knowledge of customer service. People who haven't had that experience can build this skill in other ways, like volunteering to serve as an usher at a local theater or helping at an event at a community center. Simply jotting down a list of places where one has enjoyed good or bad customer service and their characteristics can be helpful. Better yet, chat with the owner of a favorite business, like a neighborhood coffee shop, and find out how staff is trained to provide great service. YouTube can be a source of training videos from companies recognized for their customer service. People who already work at a small museum should consider asking for a quick training on the front desk procedures and should offer to step in occasionally (often enough so the skills don't get rusty).

PRIORITIZATION

It's a universal truth of non-profit work that there are not enough hours in the day to accomplish everything that needs to be done. In part, the budget creates this limitation—staffing may be bare bones—but it's also related to our impulse as a field to jump on every possible opportunity to expand our reach and deepen our relationships. This is the case for the museum as an institution as well as for nearly all employees on an individual basis. Further, much of the work is on a tight timeline: exhibitions need to open, catalogs need to go to the printer, newsletters have to be mailed, and grant applications have to be submitted. Also, as we've touched on in some of the individual jobs, multiple deadlines—short, medium, and long-term—coexist, with different levels of attention required. Additionally, because so much museum work is collaborative, people depend on each other to produce deliverables on time; for example, an exhibition can't open until the graphic designer gets the labels back from the printer. Prioritization is essential so that employees spend their time and energy on the most important projects, while also keeping an eye on deadlines and what they need to deliver to other staff.

Skill Building in Prioritization

Prioritization is a bit harder to practice than some other skills, but it can be supported by good systems. These will vary from individual to individual, but may include some combination of online and hardcopy calendars, to-do lists, reminders, or—for larger projects—project management software. People who don't have a good system in place should experiment with some options to see what works best. It's also useful for a candidate to be able to articulate in a cover letter or interview how he approaches prioritization. If this is an area where an employee (or potential employee) struggles, he should consider working with a management or productivity coach. If a coach is cost-prohibitive, there are countless books and online tools on the topic as well. One of my favorite frameworks for thinking about prioritization is Stephen Covey's quadrant model from the book *The 7 Habits of Highly Effective People.*[1] The model is a matrix of important/not important and urgent/not urgent, and has strategies for dealing for each of the four types of tasks (important and urgent, important and not urgent, not important and urgent, and not important and not urgent).

BEING PROACTIVE

Another side effect of the fact that there is never enough time for museums—or their employees—to accomplish everything they want to do is that non-urgent pursuits may get put on the back burner and stay there indefinitely. Examples of these worthwhile, or even essential, activities include professional development and training, exposure to other parts of the museum, or productive feedback outside of an annual review. Staff who want or need these things will benefit from learning to ask for them rather than waiting for them to be offered. How the staff person makes the request is crucial, though: it should be framed in terms of how the opportunity will benefit first the individual and, by extension, the institution. For example, attendance at a conference may provide an opportunity for an employee to make connections, hone a skill, or meet with museum vendors; the staff should be able to articulate how they will bring that benefit back to the museum. Requests should also be reasonable (within budget), not detract from accomplishing day-to-day tasks, and should be paced appropriately—the goal is to demonstrate a growth mind-set, not to appear needy.

While certainly many opportunities, like training, can be expensive, countless others are free: inviting a colleague in another department to have coffee, seeking out free professional development at a chamber of commerce or other community resource, or asking to sit in on a meeting in an area of interest when appropriate. Say, for example, that a junior development staff person knows that in order to progress in her career, she needs to learn about grant writing. She could sign up for a course, read journals about non-profit fundraising, and view successful grant applications on the websites of granting agencies. She could also offer to help the grant writer by proofreading applications that need another pair of eyes. In a best-case scenario, this helps both the junior staff member to gain exposure to the process and helps the grant writer polish the application and make sure it's typo-free. To repeat a caveat, junior employees should only consider this type of an arrangement if they're caught up on their own work, they check with their supervisors, they can provide some benefit to the institution through the task (the request isn't just self-serving), and they are competent in the skills they're offering (a poor speller shouldn't volunteer to proofread). One of the best things about museums is that they are institutions devoted to lifelong learning. Though this may not translate to staff as often as it should, for the most part staff who ask for opportunities thoughtfully and responsibly are likely to receive them.

Skill Building in Being Proactive

Being proactive is as much of a mind-set as a skill. To underscore a point made more than once previously, but which still bears repeating: the extent to which requests will be granted depends on the employee's competence in the job she has been hired to do. Assuming that basic requirement is met, employees should keep their eyes out for opportunities—they abound in the non-profit world, if one is open to them—and should practice saying yes. For example, an employee could offer to attend a community meeting in the place of a colleague who has a scheduling conflict. Staff may be able to go to museum events or openings for free, giving them the ability not only to enjoy the event themselves, but also to see the museum through the eyes of a visitor. If the opportunity requires permission (say, doing something outside of one's job description), the employee should write a one-page memo that anticipates his or her supervisor's questions: how much time will be required, how will the employee keep up with her other work, and how will her own department and/or the museum benefit?

CONNECTING WITH THE MISSION

One of the best ways for museum staff to remain focused, feel like they're making a difference, and avoid burnout is to focus on the mission of the museum. All museums have a mission statement that says what the museum does and how it serves its public. Some museums also have a vision statement, which is aspirational, stating what the museum hopes to be in the future; some also have a values statement, which highlights a few of the key qualities on which the museum places importance. Mission statements, and sometimes vision and values, are available on the museum's website, in the annual report, and even its non-profit tax return documents, which are publicly available.

With some museum jobs, the link to the mission is clear; with others, the link is more tangential. Regardless, all museum jobs, wherever they land on the organizational chart, exist to help the institution carry out its mission. Remembering this can make every job more rewarding and can help to mitigate some of the less-than-ideal aspects of every position.

Skill Building in Connecting with the Mission

Museum employees should take some time out of their work schedules on a regular basis—at least weekly—to experience the galleries and public spaces of the museum. This applies even to staff who regularly work in the galleries; they may spend a lot of time in the space, but probably not very often in the role of a viewer. Being able to spend time in the galleries, on the grounds, in a historic building, or otherwise taking advantage of what the museum has to offer is one of the major perks of the job, but it's all too easy for staff to feel like they shouldn't leave their desks. All staff, regardless of how busy they are, can at least find a few minutes on a lunch break to visit a favorite object or walk through a new exhibition.

All staff should take time to read the museum's strategic plan; a digest version is often available on the museum's website, and a full version should be made available to staff upon request. Since nearly all of the museum's work over the period of the plan (typically three to five years) should stem from the goals of the strategic plan, each employee should understand their role in meeting those goals.

MEASURING IMPACT

Increasingly, the multiple stakeholders of a museum—board, funders, donors, community partners—expect the museum to be able to demonstrate its impact. In short, how is the museum making a difference in its community? Funders want to know that their money is affecting positive change. Board members need to be sure the museum's resources are being used in service of the mission. Even the museum's non-profit tax status is predicated upon its betterment of the community through education and services. While everyone involved with a museum can undoubtedly tell many anecdotes about how the museum has affected them and the great things the museum has accomplished, the real challenge is capturing the data that demonstrates this impact. Museum evaluation is a huge topic—too big to do more than mention here—and is a topic that will continue to be increasingly important to institutions and museum practitioners. While not every staff member will be involved in formal evaluation, being conversant with evaluation practices may be useful for people aspiring to positions in museums.

Skill Building in Measuring Impact

Even staff who are not involved in evaluation per se can practice goal setting and soliciting feedback. This can be as simple as asking visitors what they thought about whatever part of the museum the staff person oversees (say, the front desk check-in process), or somewhat more complex, such as developing a short survey for people to fill out after a program. Note that if the museum has staff who are dedicated to evaluation, other staff should check with them before implementing any type of evaluation tool.

Staff can also keep track of their own impact in the way they set annual goals. Say, for example, a goal the membership manager pinpoints at her annual review is to increase renewal rates by 10 percent. By tracking progress and calculating impact in terms of dollars and the number of member households, the manager can become more accustomed to thinking about outcomes and how she contributes to the museum's success, and therefore to its ability to deliver the mission.

CREATIVITY

Art museums may be the first association that comes to mind when the word creativity is applied to the museum field. Certainly, art museums are wonderful places to practice creative pursuits and to be inspired by others. However, I believe that every staff member at every museum (really, at every non-profit) can benefit in their career by practicing creativity. Creativity is partly necessary because of limitations of time and money, but it can also be the spark that generates support for the museum and its mission. Some museum positions may have creativity inherent in their job descriptions, like the graphic designer, the exhibitions team, or the educator who oversees a studio art program. Beyond the obvious, it's part of every job: the finance manager who finds new ways to save money; the marketing manager who develops an ad campaign for an exhibition; the development manager who can almost magically turn a conference room into a setting for an elegant donor lunch. Cultivating and practicing creativity is one of the main ways to stay engaged with the mission of the museum, and it helps make some of the challenges of working in a museum (like tight budgets) a bit easier.

The museum where I felt the most engaged as an employee was one where creativity thrived. As just one example, the director created a cross-departmental team of four or five people who were charged with implementing a system of defining and practicing workplace values. As part of this initiative, each staff person had a cache of red thank-you cards (the same color as the museum's logo) and five dollar Starbucks cards. When a staff member saw a colleague doing something that embodied one of the museum's core values, like being smart or gracious—especially if it was a small gesture that might otherwise go unacknowledged—the staff member was encouraged to leave a thank-you note for that colleague. This creative initiative cost very little—a few hundred dollars a year for the Starbucks cards—but made an enormous impact on the workplace and ultimately on what the museum was able to accomplish.

Skill Building in Creativity

Everyone can be creative, even if they don't think of themselves that way. Set aside time on a daily, weekly, or monthly basis to do something—anything—creative: try a new recipe, practice a hobby (sewing, woodworking, playing an instrument, gardening), write someone a letter, plan a party, experiment with art supplies. Think about the process, not the outcome, and define creativity broadly: any activity in which a person uses their hands to make something new.

For people who need more structure, try a challenge. For example, say the development department needs to decorate for a holiday reception. Rather than calling in a florist, which is expensive, they could challenge themselves to come up with centerpieces that cost less than three dollars each. (I've seen this done to great effect with clear glass vases and dollar-store Christmas ornaments.)

An important part of creativity is leaving some mental space to let the mind wander and to let ideas percolate. This space is harder and harder to come by as we become more dependent on technology, but it's worth pursuing it. Try driving to work without the radio or a podcast playing or observing a periodic screen-free day or week.

PATHWAYS TO MUSEUM WORK

One of the reasons museums are interesting places to work is that people come from so many backgrounds. With the exception of conservation, which has a strictly prescribed set of credentials, people can come to museum work through many different avenues. We'll look at three possible paths in a general sense here. Note, though, that strict delineations are artificial—often these paths overlap or intersect, though one is usually primary.

By Discipline

Perhaps the most traditional way of approaching a job in a museum is through the discipline or content area of the museum. This path usually entails academic work in art history, science, natural history, geology, anthropology, or a related field. Curators often follow this path, but it could also apply to almost any other position in the museum—anyone who needed an answer to that dreaded question "What are you going to do with that history [or art history or anthropology or . . .] degree?"

People who follow the discipline path typically get a BA and an MA in their field, with a PhD often preferred for curatorial positions. Practical experience in museums, often achieved through internships, is also required. An individual might start at a junior level initially, earning an advanced degree concurrently with working, or going back to school full-time after having worked for a few years.

A strictly academic path likely does not include training in management, supervision, budgeting, strategic planning, or other necessary skills for museum leaders. People who come to museums through this inroad need to find other ways to build these skills in order to be competitive and to be successful in the job. Content specialists who don't have—and aren't willing to acquire—management skills can be a real liability for the museum. Therefore, content specialists who are also good managers are highly desirable.

By Role

People may come to museums through the role or job they wish to have rather than through the discipline. Another way to put it is that these people may think first about the role and second about the museum context. These could be people who are skilled in marketing, information technology, education, fundraising, human resources, graphic design, or any number of other types of vocations. These people may have always intended to work in museums, or they may come to museums unexpectedly, say, if a course, internship, or part-time job helps them to discover the museum field.

The specifics of this path vary greatly, depending on the requirements of the position. In many cases, a BA is required, though the area of study can be fairly broad at the undergraduate level. An MA is often preferred and is the point where the field of study narrows and becomes goal-oriented. Museum studies degrees are one option, though if an MA is required or preferred, the field is often not specified (that is, an MA in museum education could be perceived as equal to an MA in art history).

A generation ago, museum studies programs might have been considered a "lesser" path than the academic path. Thankfully, that elitist view has changed, and museum studies programs are appropriately recognized for offering certificates and degrees that teach valuable skills and theory, sending well-prepared students into the museum workforce.[2]

Traditionally, directors tended to follow the academic track, but now they come from a wider variety of other fields, such as other non-profits or universities. Directors, especially of large and jumbo institutions, are likely to have extensive business experience and may have an MBA instead of, or in addition to, a content-specific degree.

By Happy Accident

The lure of museums draws talented people from almost every field imaginable. These are people who initially practiced their vocation elsewhere and for various reasons pivot toward museums. This could be based on relocation, a job loss, or other outside circumstance, or it could be because the individual's current workplace is no longer desirable, possibly for lifestyle reasons like a lack of schedule flexibility or a long commute. Examples here are endless: classroom teachers who become museum educators; artists who need regular income and benefits and so work as preparators; graphic designers or marketing specialists who come from advertising.

This path has pros and cons for the field. On the pro side, staff who are experienced in other settings can bring new perspectives and ideas to museums. This can be quite important for keeping museums from being too insular. On the con side, as this book attests, museums are idiosyncratic workplaces; even if an individual uses the same skills she used at another job, she'll still have a learning curve coming in to a museum.

CHOOSING A PATH

At almost every museum, the staff will be composed of people from each of these three paths, people who are all enjoying a similar level of success in their careers. That is, no one path is inherently better than the others, though each has its pros and cons. Ultimately the decision requires a balance of two factors and the answers to the questions that they evoke. The first factor to consider is the investment of time and money required to earn the relevant degrees or credentials and to complete the necessary internships. Questions to ask include: What is the anticipated entry-level salary relative to the amount of student loans? What is the cost of living in the places where the job seeker is hoping to settle? Given other circumstances related to family considerations, the job seeker's age, or other similar factors, is it practical or desirable to spend the time required to get a particular degree or credential? If the answer is no, what other possible inroad could lead to a museum job?

The second factor is the level of certainty about staying in a particular role in the museum field. Questions to ask include: Does the job seeker have enough information to commit to the specific type of job? Do they have experience and do they know what it's really like on a day-to-day basis? What is plan B if, for whatever reason, the target job isn't available or doesn't fit with some aspect of the job seeker's life at a later point? Are there transferable skills or other ways one's training could be applied? My best advice in determining a path is to remain as flexible as possible for as long as possible, and to develop the skills discussed in the first part of this chapter. That approach provides an equally good foundation for people who land their dream jobs and for people who—for circumstances related to the workplace or for personal or family considerations—need to shift a bit or need to make a complete 180-degree switch.

13

Things I Wish I Had Known When I Was Twenty-Four

Opportunities and Challenges

Like many people in the field, I began my first full-time job soon after I finished graduate school. I was twenty-four. I had a BA and an MA in art history, had completed at least four internships, and had worked part-time at my university's museum throughout college. I was ready for an adventure, and I excitedly but a little nervously packed up my parents' old station wagon and drove across country to start my new job. With my internships and part-time work, I had a fairly good idea of what to expect. In fact, the person who would be my supervisor in this new job had also been my supervisor at one of my internships, so we already had a good working relationship.

My parents co-signed the lease on a tiny but charming studio apartment. The pay was low, but workable; it could cover my rent, gas, utilities, bus pass, groceries, and regular payments on my undergraduate loans (mercifully, I didn't have any from graduate school because I had worked as a teaching assistant). The museum offered health insurance, a 403b retirement account (without a match), and a pension—which is unheard of now outside of government or university museums. I was lucky: though my salary covered most living expenses, my family could help with plane tickets home for the holidays and other unexpected expenses.

I loved my job, and I was able to get by on the low salary, even in an expensive city. While I thought I understood a lot about how museums worked, I had focused mostly on the art content. I didn't fully comprehend the scope of the other parts of a curator's job; for example, especially in the contemporary art world, curators spend a lot of time in the social realm, at exhibition openings, art fairs, studio visits, and so forth. As an introvert, this did not come naturally to me, and I began to realize, over time, that aspects of the curator role were not a good fit. Because I had wanted to be a curator since I was in high school, this realization felt devastating. The happy ending to this anecdote is that this feeling of disconnect spurred me to move into museum education, which turned out to be the right path for me.

I'm telling this story to illustrate my goal of helping prospective museum employees think through some of the implications of museum work that may not be apparent, or that seem unimportant as a twenty-something, but can dramatically impact the course of one's life in the decades to follow. Some of these points I've touched on in previous areas of the book, but they are worth re-emphasizing. There are opportunities to consider, and challenges as well. However, I'm not framing these as pros and cons; they're simply factors to think about. Each of them will have different implications for different people.

OPPORTUNITIES

Lifelong Learning and Travel

Whether or not a museum employee spends her days working on content-related projects, *all* museum employees—even those behind the scenes—work at an educational institution. Opportunities to take advantage of educational enrichment are nearly endless. At some institutions, such opportunities might be designed especially for staff. For example, a curator might give a staff tour of an exhibition before it opens to the public. At one small museum I worked at, the entire staff went on regular outings to other museums in the region to meet their employees, see how the museum operated, and to generate new ideas for our own institution.

Even if there aren't activities geared exclusively toward staff, at most institutions employees can attend museum programs—lectures, films, workshops, concerts—for free or at a discounted rate. Though there might be restrictions or limitations if the event is particularly popular with the public or expensive to produce, nearly every museum has a diverse roster of programs to enjoy. Generally speaking, larger museums have more to choose from, but they're also more likely to have restrictions on staff attendance due to the numbers of people who want to participate.

Travel is also another way that museum employees can learn on the job. These opportunities are more limited to those staff who work directly with exhibitions and programs; oftentimes curators will travel to see objects, exhibition designers will visit other museums to see traveling exhibitions in advance of hosting them, and registrars or collection managers will serve as couriers for outgoing loans. However, broader opportunities may be possible. For example, the museum store manager might attend regional or national gift shows to see trending products and meet with vendors. An educator might travel to another museum to help train interpreters on a traveling exhibition originating from her home institution. These opportunities depend on the scope of the museum's work and the size of the budget, but they're worth seeking out as a perk of working at a museum.

It's important for museum employees to visit other museums to stay up to date on what is happening within the field. Fortunately, there are ways to do this for free or at a very low cost. The American Alliance of Museums (AAM) and its regional affiliates have reciprocal admission agreements among member museums, usually offering free admission for the employee and sometimes a guest as well. Though not as widely publicized, many museums offer free admission for staff who show proof of employment at another museum; policies vary, but in some cases this applies to the entire party, not just the employee.

In my more than twenty years of working in museums, I've enjoyed some unbelievable learning opportunities for little to no out-of-pocket cost. I've met famous artists, had books signed by well-known writers, visited amazing private collections, taken workshops in painting and basket making, heard lectures from some of the leading professionals in the field, been in collection storage at the Metropolitan Museum of Art and more than one of the Smithsonians, traveled on both coasts and in between, and seen scores—if not hundreds—of films, concerts, readings, and performances. Admittedly, some of these experiences were unique to my roles in curatorial and education, but most of the ones I list here, and many others not listed, were available to a broad range of employees from a variety of departments.

Making a Difference

By definition, museums exist to make a positive impact on their communities by serving primarily as educational institutions. This means that every employee—regardless of her role—is involved in creating that impact. Increasingly, museums are becoming more vital partners in their communities: no longer elitist institutions for the few, but welcoming and accessible institutions for the many. All employees can take pride in that fact.

I want to take a moment to talk about "passion" here; in my opinion, passion is an overused term in the non-profit world, and is a notion that is all too often used to justify poor pay. Following one's passion and making a living wage are not mutually exclusive; a surgeon might be following his passion and also making hundreds of thousands of dollars. Personally, I find the idea of impact much more meaningful; it gives me a sense of purpose, and it's a concept that focuses my energy outward—to the community—rather than inward to my own interests.

As a museum professional, sometimes I've struggled with the idea of impact, especially as I've become more interested in the non-profit sector beyond the museum field and seen the direct and immediate impact that other types of non-profits have, especially social services. I took a non-profit management course with a cohort of non-profit professionals who were mainly from the social services sector, and I was continually amazed by what they were doing in their day-to-day work: they were literally saving lives through their work with families experiencing domestic violence, gang-affiliated individuals, and children being treated for malnutrition. In this milieu, I admit I found it challenging to think about my museum's impact, but a course assignment to write a "pitch" for a prospective funder helped me to articulate what it is that museums do best: celebrate human creativity and achievement, connect people to each other, help people cultivate empathy, build skills in critical thinking, and have a positive economic impact on our neighborhoods and communities, just to name a few. These achievements can be hard to measure, but they're evident in our day-to-day work if we take a moment to look.

At the risk of sounding cliché, I know that the vast majority of museum staff who interact with the public—and even staff whose relationship to the visitor is less direct—can pinpoint moments when they have thought "*This* is why I work at a museum." I'll share my own favorite example. The small art museum where I worked for several years had a partnership with the sixth graders at the local middle school. Because many of the students had never been to any art museum, and because the content of the collection was esoteric, helping the students find points of entry could be challenging. Our goals were not to teach specific collection-related content, but to introduce the kids to this world-class museum a mile away from their school, and to begin to make connections between ways artists used symbols to convey information and how the kids would use a similar system of symbols in an upcoming school project. One morning, the docents and I welcomed about sixty sixth graders for a ninety-minute visit, as we had done many times before. Something that had *never* happened before took place later that afternoon at about 3:30, a half hour before we closed: one of the boys from the morning group brought his mom to the museum to show her what he had learned that morning. We'd had students return with families before, but never the same day: the timing meant that he had been picked up from school and immediately asked his mom to take him right to the museum. He arrived with a remarkable sense of urgency; he had to share this experience with his mom right away. We let them both in for free and allowed them to stay after closing. This was one of those moments for me, where I could see the impact that the museum experience had on this family—not just that afternoon, but likely for a long time to come.

Joining an Instant Network

Every field has dedicated, creative individuals who excel at their jobs and work together to build a professional community, but museum people seem to have an extra spark that they bring to their relationships with colleagues. Perhaps it's related to the creativity inherent in many museum jobs, the sense of shared mission, or the fact that we prioritize workplace culture over money (if we prioritized money, we'd be in a different field). The museum community is incredibly welcoming, helpful, and networked, and every museum staff person—including prospective staffers—can take part in it.

Let's look at a few examples of what I mean; the following examples are not only common, but they're also encouraged, for staff at all levels. An entry-level staff person can happen to sit down next to a senior museum professional (say a director at a large museum) at the AAM annual meeting and conference and strike up a conversation, resulting in the exchange of business cards; a museum staff person planning to travel to nearly any museum in the country can, with one email or phone call, connect with an employee at that museum and undoubtedly be invited for coffee, lunch, or a meet and greet, even though the two individuals have never met; a prospective museum employee can ask for—and be granted—an informational interview with almost any museum staff person at any level.

The relationships that one can build within the museum community not only make the work more enjoyable, but they also create opportunities for advancement. The conversations at conferences and the cups of coffee with colleagues can lead to all sorts of possibilities—from collaboration on projects to leads on jobs. Perhaps more importantly, they can lead to lifelong friendships and to colleagues who are just a call, email, or text away whenever one needs advice or someone to listen. Two caveats about these networks: first, though they may indeed advance one's career, that's a bonus, not the reason to build them in the first place. In fact, though these kinds of insider relationships could improve one's prospects in the job hunt, they also perpetuate a lack of diversity in the field; AAM, for example, has adopted a blind hiring process in which candidates' names are not visible on the initial application materials, to make the process more equitable. Still, whether or not they advance one's career, these networks are worth building. The second caveat is that one must be willing to pay the generosity forward. Though it probably seems far away, the entry-level museum employees requesting informational interviews today will be the senior staff people on the other side of the desk at some point. Networks of museum people work best when everyone gives their best input and guidance to colleagues without expecting anything in return.

Forging a Personal Path

Because people come to museum work through so many different avenues, and because creativity is a key value, the field tends to be open to allowing people to forge their own paths. This doesn't necessarily mean one can bypass usual processes and create new jobs. But it does mean that an innovative person who does excellent work can create new opportunities for herself. This creativity is one way that a new employee can deal with some of the limitations of the job search: by taking a less-than-ideal job (perhaps even a part-time one), proving herself, and building it into something more. While this is not a sure bet, and while it doesn't solve some of the real employment problems or inequities in the field, I have seen it happen many times. Forging one's own path may be more about combining or showcasing a unique set of skills than creating a new job opportunity, or it may be both. Some real-life examples: a person with an art history degree and a customer service background who successfully proposed combining a part-time visitor services position and a part-time curatorial assistant job into one full-time position; a museum custodian with an amazing singing voice who was often hired, with her band, to perform at special museum events; interns who made themselves so indispensable that they were hired at their host museums upon graduation; an individual with an extensive personal collection of sports memorabilia who donated the collection to a history museum and served as a consulting curator for the collection's installation.

Sometimes one forges a new path through projects within an existing position. As we discussed in the section of chapter 12 about being proactive, opportunities abound for people who want them; this is true at virtually every museum, because there are always more possible projects than there are staff. In most institutions, if someone is willing to exercise creativity and take a new project on, the institution will be supportive, provided the time and budget permit. Say, for example, that the marketing manager at a small museum also serves as the graphic designer. She notices that one of the education department's gallery activity sheets has good content, but is visually bland, printed in black ink on regular copy paper. With the input of the education manager, the marketing manager could offer to design a new version of the activity sheet. Not only does this small project enhance the visitor experience by offering audiences a more attractive and user-friendly handout, but it also better showcases the educator's work and gives the marketing manager another piece to add to her portfolio—and even to submit to AAM's publication award competition. This type of project can be done for a relatively small investment of time and money, yet it can make a difference for the institution while providing a professional boost for the staff.

CHALLENGES

Compensation

Perhaps the most notable challenge is the relatively low pay in the museum field. There are structural problems that perpetuate the salary issue: for example, many museums base their pay scale on comparables in the field, without accounting for the fact that these comparables are reports of actual depressed salaries. That is, by using comparables, managers are situating salaries within a framework that is already low, not within one that accounts for where salaries should be.

Low starting salaries are only one factor of compensation. In my experience, in private non-profit museums, raises are infrequent and sporadic. Cost-of-living increases of 2 percent or 3 percent are not even a given. Additionally, employees often pay a substantial share of health care costs. Retirement funds, if available, are not matched as they are in the private sector.

The issue to consider here is not just the level of one's entering salary—people new to the field often anticipate having to live a fairly spartan existence, say, with several roommates. There are more significant considerations to the salary issue: having to have a second job, for instance, has a major impact on the amount of energy one can devote to museum work. The salary issues become more striking when one enters a different life stage, and the income becomes less workable for various reasons. A few examples: wanting to live alone or with a partner rather than with roommates, planning to buy a house, having kids and wanting to move to a bigger space or a better school district, not having enough saved for retirement, or taking unpaid maternity leave and needing to figure out how to recover financially from that loss of income. In short, prospective museum employees need to think about the financial implications of a career in museums, not just that first job.

I recommend not just being resigned to the low salary or to justify it with the excuse of following a passion, but doing some substantive research. There are several ways to do this: run some numbers in a cost of living calculator, get an estimate of how much retirement savings will be required, and calculate the monthly payments for student loans and the end date of the loan. Industry salary surveys give some information, but again, keep in mind that these numbers reflect actual museum salaries, which are already low. The good news is that at long last there is some movement from within the field to address the salary issue. We'll discuss this further in chapter 14.

Another significant obstacle to stability in the museum field is the proliferation of part-time jobs. Many museums are structured so that their current budgets only allow them to hire hourly staff for certain positions, such as interpreters or visitor services staff. Part-time hours are often capped below the point at which museums would have to pay overtime and/or offer benefits. While part-time jobs do sometimes become full-time jobs, or enable a move to a full-time job in another department, part-time museum staff often need to find another museum job or a job outside of the field to make a reasonable livelihood.

Sadly, the pay issue is one of the main barriers to entering the museum field. People who don't have some sort of financial safety net—such as family to give or lend money, or a spouse or partner contributing to the household income—may not be able to live on the low pay; though they may be able to stick it out for a few years, ultimately the quality of life issues may become too big to surmount. A related challenge is the field's reliance on unpaid internships. The expectation that a student can work without compensation perpetuates the lack of diversity in the field, because it excludes lower income people, who are disproportionately people of color. Students who do internships for credit often have to pay course fees at their college or university for the opportunity to work at that unpaid internship, compounding the problem. Like with the pay issue, unpaid internships are finally coming under scrutiny as being unethical and antithetical to the field's stated goals of inclusion.

Geography

Location and mobility is an issue we've touched on before in the book, but it's another one that bears repeating here. In my case, this was something I didn't think about beyond my first cross-country move. Unless an employee works in one of the major US cities that is home to many museums of all sizes, ascending to a more senior job may require a move. This is related not only to the competitiveness of the field, but on an individual's own specialization—the more narrow, the less transferable. Anecdotally, I can say that many of the museum professionals I know whose careers progressed relatively quickly upon a linear path are people who have moved from state to state several times in their careers.

Sometimes the issue related to relocation is not that someone is following a job, but that they need to move for another reason, and then face the challenge of searching for a job within a limited geographic area. For example, an individual's spouse or partner might be offered a job in a new location; a spouse or partner who works outside of the museum field may be the main source of income in the household, meaning that their job has to take priority for financial reasons. A move might be desirable to be closer to family or for other personal reasons. Certainly there are people who stay in the same city or geographic area and who find jobs with increasing seniority either in the same institution or in another close by. If that doesn't seem likely, employees might choose to stay in the field in a couple of ways. They can decide they are willing to move if the right job comes up or they can move for another reason and hope to find another museum job in the new location. Conversely, employees may decide that leaving the field is the best option, again for a couple of reasons: they don't necessarily want to relocate but have exhausted the museum options in the immediate area, or they relocate for a personal reason but aren't able to find a job in the field, and instead pivot to another type of work. Early in one's career, when one may not have a lot of financial and family commitments, it can be exciting to live in different parts of the country and try new adventures. As one puts down roots in a community, though, moving can be less desirable for any number of reasons: a mortgage, a spouse or partner with a good job, kids in school, family nearby, or simply getting to a stage in life where relocation isn't desirable. There are also financial costs to moving, which the hiring museum may not be able to pay.

While the relocation issue isn't something that the field can change, it's still something that prospective museum employees can think about. It's important not only to contemplate the location of the first job, but also to consider what one's family and financial obligations might look like in the future. It may be desirable to set a long-term goal of ending up in a specific area in ten years or so, but to decide that moving is acceptable until then. Or, someone who knows they don't want to move may think about choosing a job in a major metropolitan area and building skills that will enable her to work remotely or independently down the road.

To continue my anecdote from the beginning of this chapter as it relates to geography, after about seven years on the West Coast, my husband and I decided that we wanted to move back to the East Coast, to a place where both sides of the family were within driving distance. We had grown tired of spending a large chunk of our disposable income and much of our time off flying across the country for holidays and family events. I was lucky enough to find a job on the East Coast less than a year after having made that decision, but it meant my husband was unemployed for a bit, and we lived with relatives for several months after we moved. It worked out well in the end, but the transition period was stressful, and I took a pay cut to land at a job in our desired location. Again, I had never really thought about this on the cross-country trip that brought me to my first full-time job. I'm not sure I would have done anything differently if I had considered the location issue, but having thought it through earlier than I did would have reduced my stress level when I arrived at that decision point later on.

Work Schedule

Another issue related to work/life/family balance is the need, in many museum jobs, to be available outside of a nine-to-five, Monday through Friday schedule. It's common sense that most people who visit museums do so outside of their own work hours. Though certainly many people visit museums during the week (especially school groups), most casual visitors who are not retired attend in the evenings and on weekends. Museum employees who work with these audiences will need to be available during those times. This includes not only frontline staff (admissions, visitor services, shop, café), but also educators, curators, and development staff. For frontline staff, they may have a regular schedule of evening, weekend, or even—in the case of security—overnight hours. For education, curatorial, and development staff, night and weekend hours are likely not part of their typical workweek, but probably still occur on a regular basis. Some educators who work in public spaces may have a shifted week, say Tuesday through Saturday, with Sunday and Monday off. Programs, openings, events, receptions, and similar events require some number of staff to be on hand to oversee the event; staff may even *be* the main attraction, like a curator giving a lecture about an exhibition.

Some additional hours like these are to be expected and should be part of the job description for the relevant roles. Though policies will vary about so-called comp time, salaried jobs are typically structured so that, at least in theory, extra hours worked can be made up elsewhere in the schedule. Say, for example, that an educator usually leaves work at five o'clock, but she stays until nine o'clock on a given night to oversee a program. Whether or not it is published in the museum's handbook, standard practice says that she can take four hours off elsewhere in the week. For instance, she might arrive at work at noon the next day or take an afternoon off later in the week.

While that approach works in theory, and often in practice, there are many times that it isn't realistic. This is especially the case in small museums, where staff may be spread thin. In the example we just used, perhaps the educator can't come in at noon the next day because, in addition to her late night program, she has a school group arriving first thing the following morning. There may not be any time within the pay period when she feels it's possible to take the time off. If this happens occasionally, then there is little cause for concern. But if an individual is regularly working significantly more than her scheduled work time and doesn't feel like she can take any time off to balance out her hours, then resentment and burnout are real risks.

Prospective museum employees should also think about how working a nonstandard schedule, or frequent nights and weekends in addition to traditional work hours, will impact other aspects of their lives. If such a work schedule conflicts with the hours that an employee's family and friends are available, the situation may not be sustainable long term. On the other hand, there may be advantages to a nonstandard work schedule. I've often heard museum staff who work Tuesday through Saturday say that they enjoy having one weekday off to run errands and go to appointments that are hard to schedule on the weekend.

For me, the night and weekend work was fine at the beginning of my career. In fact, it was fun, because the activities that filled those hours were enjoyable, and in some cases presented exciting opportunities, like travel. Later, though, it became more burdensome, especially once my kids got to the age where attending a program on a Saturday meant missing a soccer game.

The possibility of extended hours, or a non-standard regular schedule, is not inherently a negative thing. Its impact on one's work and personal life depends on many factors. Some people need more structure, and some like a lot of variety. Some people have family demands that make irregular schedules difficult, whereas other families may prefer having options; for example, the overnight shift might work well for a security guard whose spouse works days, enabling the family to save on daycare costs. While some of these factors aren't possible to determine early in one's career, being aware of them can help a prospective museum employee make an informed decision about a particular job offer.

The opportunities described in this chapter are some of the main reasons that I love working in museums despite the challenges discussed here. These opportunities don't just happen, though—most of them require being proactive and cultivating trust in one's own skills and instincts. As for the challenges, I don't intend for them to be discouraging. Rather, I present them so that prospective museum employees can think them through and can begin, as early as possible, to plan for the challenges that might be most problematic. This can be done in small steps or in big leaps; it might mean starting a retirement account as soon as one gets that first job, rather than putting it off because retirement seems so far away; it might mean choosing a less expensive graduate school or one that provides a stipend for working as a teaching or research assistant. Some of the challenges can't be avoided, and other factors are unknown. Still, thinking through which circumstances described in this chapter are deal breakers and which are acceptable not only makes it easier to make career decisions, but it also helps the employee feel less resentful.

Think about the quality of life difference between two hypothetical museum employees: one has given a lot of thought to her personal priorities; in order to avoid a stressful and expensive commute, she accepts a job at an institution that is closer to her home but that requires periodic weekend work. The other employee accepted a job that also requires weekend work, but, not having really considered how that would impact his life, ends up feeling bitter every time his friends make Saturday plans without him. The first employee had to make a tradeoff, but in doing so, she's taking control of her work situation based on her priorities, which makes her more likely to enjoy her job and be successful at it. The second employee is starting to feel like a victim of some of the challenges of museum work and is in a situation where he feels helpless. Not only have I seen both of these types of museum employees, but I've *been* both of them; I hope this chapter helps readers focus on choosing which of the challenges they can't cope with and which are a small price to pay for the ability to enjoy all of the good things about working in museums.[1]

14

Where Are Museums Going?

There are many theories and predictions about how museums are changing and what they'll look like decades in the future. The American Alliance of Museums' (AAM's) Center for the Future of Museums publishes a weekly newsletter and other excellent content, including an imagined issue of *Museum* magazine published in 2040. While some of these theories are fascinating to think about, and I encourage prospective museum employees to read about them, in this chapter we'll focus on the future museum as a workplace; that is, what will it be like to work in museums in five or ten years? What can we expect?

It seems like a contradiction, but it's true: the museum field seems to change quickly, yet it can also be glacially slow to fully adopt new ways of operating. Most of the trends I'll discuss in this chapter are, frankly, significantly overdue; museums need to play catch-up. However, there is evidence we've finally reached the tipping point, and that real progress will be made in the coming years, even if it's slower than we might like. What gives me great hope is the commitment to equity and advocacy evidenced by so many "emerging museum professionals"; we can credit them for much of the progress that has been made. People just entering the field need to make their voices heard as well, as the future of the profession.

A NEW GENERATION OF LEADERSHIP

The museum field is at a turning point: the Baby Boom generation (born between 1946 and 1964) has been leading the field for decades but its members are now retiring at a rapid rate. This means that a new generation of leaders is taking the reins; both Generation Xers (born between 1965 and 1980) and Millennials (born between 1981 and 1996) are assuming the roles that Boomers are vacating. While it's difficult to make general statements about any generation, there are some distinctive differences between Boomers and GenXers that may create noticeable change in the workplace.

While Boomers have tended to stay for long stretches in relatively few museums, younger generations are more used to moving between jobs after shorter durations of employment. As the Boomers phase out of the workplace, museums will be losing their employees with the most longevity and institutional knowledge.[1] The field will need to determine ways to become more used to hiring and onboarding quickly, and creating ways to retain institutional knowledge.

What are the implications of a generational shift in leadership for people entering the field? First, more jobs may open up as Boomers retire and the remaining generations move up the ranks. Second, leadership will likely become less "top down" and more collaborative, as preferred by Generation X and Millennials. Overall, based on generalized characteristics, the generations that are moving into leadership as the Boomers retire tend to be less hierarchical, more committed to finding work/life balance, and more interested in an engaging and enjoyable work environment—all things that suggest a happier workplace on the horizon. I highly recommend reading more about generational dynamics in the workplace; not only is it a fascinating topic, but it also provides some useful insight into management styles and employee culture. In particular, there are significant generational differences in communication style; understanding these can make one's daily work life smoother.

EQUITY AND DIVERSITY

Currently, the museum field is far from diverse. According to a 2015 Mellon Foundation report, 72 percent of staff at museums that are members of the Association of Art Museum Directors are non-Hispanic white, and 28 percent are historically underrepresented minorities. Looking specifically at staff comprising leadership, curator, conservator, and educator roles, 84 percent are non-Hispanic white, 6 percent Asian, 4 percent black, 3 percent Hispanic white, and 3 percent two or more races.[2] While this particular study looked only at art museums, we can assume that the numbers are similar across the museum field at large. Clearly, these percentages do not reflect the demographic make-up of the United States' population, which means that there are many people in our communities who do not see themselves represented in the leadership, staff, or even in the collections of the museum.

Effecting change in this area is a frustratingly slow process due to two factors: one, the leadership of museums for the past few decades has been dominated by Baby Boomers, who were a less diverse generation; and two, to foster diversity, we need to reexamine—and rebuild—the entire structure of the field, which is no small undertaking. For example, the perceived requirement of completing several unpaid internships perpetuates a lack of diversity. Fortunately, we're starting to see movement on this particular issue: there is an increasingly broad effort across the field to eliminate unpaid internships to help create access for people who are currently underrepresented in the field.

DEAI—diversity, equity, access, and inclusion—is one of the focus areas in AAM's current strategic plan, as a topic that its membership "strongly believes [is] vital to the future viability, relevance, and sustainability of museums."[3] Toward this end, AAM has convened a DEAI working group to examine issues of inequity in the field and make recommendations for how they can be addressed. One example is AAM's own recent commitment to a blind hiring process, whereby candidates' identifying information is removed from applications in the first stages of review.

There is also an increasing awareness of the importance of recruiting diverse boards, and of making sure that all communities see themselves reflected in the institution—through the staff, the collections, the interpretation, and the programming. Over the next several years, prospective or new employees to the field will see board and staff become more diverse, and will see increasingly diverse stories and perspectives told through objects, exhibitions, and programs. As these practices are put into place and communicated to the public, museums' visitorship will hopefully become more diverse as well.

Equity has come to the forefront of the conversations around museum leadership in terms of gender as well as racial and ethnic background. The group Gender Equity in Museums Movement (GEMM) is doing some important work raising awareness of gender imbalance in museums and advocating for change through means like salary transparency. The GEMM website and the book *Women in Museums*, by two of GEMM's founders, Anne Ackerson and Joan Baldwin, are essential resources for all leaders in the field, not just women. Tremendous progress still needs to be made in terms of gender equity; conversations like the ones taking place through GEMM—the first I've seen truly catch on in my twenty years in the field—are a crucial first step.

EMPLOYEE WELL-BEING

Museums have spent the last twenty years or so becoming more connected to their communities. However, for far too long, they have not prioritized their most immediate and most committed community: their staff.

The elephant in the room—low pay—is finally being addressed in a meaningful way. Some museum-focused professional associations are requiring job listings on their sites to publish salaries in their job advertisements, and there is a call for other associations to follow suit. Not only does publishing salaries save museums and candidates time (because people for whom the salary is too low won't apply), but it also means that the two parties start from the same place in salary negotiations. There is a growing awareness of the need to look outside of the field for benchmarking, such as using a cost-of-living calculator and other tools rather than relying solely on comparable salaries from within the field.[4] Authors Dawn E. Salerno and Mark S. Gold have called for a "new paradigm" of employee compensation:

> Compensation policies are designed to attract and retain the best employees to yield the best programming and visitor experience, while at the same time meeting mission and revenue goals.[5] Equitable pay is a mission-critical investment in, and ultimately the path towards, the museum's success.[6]

For the first time that I am aware of, a forthcoming publication will be devoted entirely to a discussion of the salary issue in museums. This in itself is a huge step forward in addressing the problem.

Simply put, it's short-sighted for museums to only think about the bottom line when looking at compensation. Overworked, underpaid employees often experience barriers to doing their best work: worry or stress about finances, long commutes to and from affordable communities, a second job that diverts their energy and attention, difficulty paying back student loans, cutting corners in relation to health and self-care, and general burnout. Paying people more won't solve all of these problems, but it will help, and it will ultimately lead to a more productive workforce that is focused, committed, less stressed, and less likely to leave—saving the institution the costs of high turnover.

The pushback in the field comes from the notion that the funds just don't exist to pay people more, to offer benefits, or to transition part-time staff to full-time. Certainly there are financial considerations that could have their own effects on the workplace, such as an increased focus on earned income, or a reduction in the number of staff so that their pay can be improved. It's difficult to say if or when we'll see measurable change in this area, but I'm gratified that for the first time in my career the issue seems to be at the forefront of the conversation.

Other aspects related to employee well-being are being discussed too, things like the importance of taking time off, leadership's responsibility to set an example about work/life boundaries (directors: don't send emails to your staff at 2 a.m.), creating mentorship opportunities, and so forth. In 2017, an informal survey discussed on the AAM blog looked at some of the reasons people leave the museum field and found that low pay was the primary reason, but certainly not the only one.[7] A lack of available jobs and an imbalance between work and non-work time were others. The post offered solutions both for individuals and for management.

CONTINUED PROFESSIONALIZATION

Another factor related to the issue of compensation is the field's heavy reliance on volunteers to perform a significant portion of the frontline work, mostly in the form of tours. While volunteers bring enormous benefits to the museum in terms of their time, networks, and, in many cases, financial support, such a reliance on volunteers has the unintended effect of diminishing the actual and perceived value of staff, especially educators. Whether or not it's conscious, the thought process inherent in this scenario is as follows: if volunteers will do the work for free, why should the museum pay people to give tours?

This way of thinking is a vestige of the time, several decades ago, where education was considered an ancillary function; volunteers were historically the ones who created museum education departments and established the field. Now, though, I strongly believe the time has come to put well-trained paid staff on the frontlines giving tours. This function is absolutely essential to the mission of the museum, and to not invest in it seems not only counterintuitive but also self-defeating.

Many museums already use paid interpreters rather than volunteers, and more and more museums are moving in this direction. I believe that the trend toward further professionalization of the interpreter role will continue, both because of the pay equity issue and because there will be a natural generational transition. Certainly museums can and should continue to use volunteers, just not in such a mission-critical role.

What does this mean for prospective staff? Ideally it will mean that there will be a greater need for paid educators, if and when volunteer interpreters are phased out of educator roles. It's hard to say when we'll be on the other side of the transition, or if it will mean more full-time, benefited jobs or just more part-time ones without benefits. The increased expenses museums will incur if they transition from volunteer to paid interpreters may require budget cuts elsewhere. This change may also mean there will be higher expectations of interpreters who are paid, which could translate into an actual or perceived graduate school requirement. Ultimately, though, further professionalizing the interpreter role will be beneficial for staff and for visitors.

FINANCIAL REALISM

Since the economic recovery after the 2008 financial crisis, there seems to be a greater sense of realism in the museum field about the importance of financial stability, not just for the present, but also to ensure that the museum's work is sustainable in the future. Taking a hard look at an institution's financial prospects is not an easy process, and in many cases it has led to decisions to close museums, to reorganize their structure, or to merge ("integrate" seems to be the preferred term). Just in the last five years in my immediate area I've seen three museums cease functioning as independent entities, integrating with larger organizations to ensure sustainability of parts of the collection, site, and programs of the smaller museum.

While the demise or restructuring of a museum can be painful for the community, not to mention staff who lose jobs, this practice of introspection will make museums stronger in the long run. It's better, and more fiscally responsible, for a museum to make strategic cuts that enable it to survive than for it to continue to stretch itself financially to keep the status quo. For example, let's imagine that a mid-size museum has a temporary exhibition gallery that hosts three traveling special exhibitions per year, each for a four-month duration. After conducting some financial modeling and seeing a troublesome financial picture ten or twenty years out, the board and the director might make a strategic decision to instead host one major special exhibition per year for a six-month duration, and fill the gallery with objects from its own collection for the remaining six months. Though this will be a noticeable—and probably disappointing—change for the community, it could save the museum hundreds of thousands of dollars annually, making for a much brighter financial picture in ten or twenty years. The caveat here is not to cut back so much on the museum's mission-critical work that audience numbers start to fall off, which has its own negative financial consequences. Strategic financial decisions like this example have to be made thoughtfully and approached with creativity to figure out how to maintain community engagement.

For people who are in the museum workforce when these types of cuts are made, the changes can be difficult—jobs can change focus, be reconfigured, or eliminated entirely. If these decisions are made carefully and the financial resources are stewarded appropriately, the next generation of staff will ideally come in to more stable institutions. One of my former colleagues told me that she felt constant personal stress when the institution we worked for was financially unstable—not because she thought she was going to lose her job, necessarily, but because the atmosphere was tense, and because she felt the weight of every decision she made, even in terms of deciding whether she should buy certain supplies required for her job. If today's museum leaders can make the hard decisions to make museums more stable, museums in the future will be able to come out from under this type of stress, making museums happier and more productive places to work.

COMMUNITY FOCUS

Museums can only become more diverse and remain financially stable if they engage their communities. While museums have long served their communities, they are now finding more ways to be relevant to people outside of the usual visitor profile (that is, to non-visitors) and more ways to connect to the community's real needs, not just to what museums *think* communities want. To share just a few of the many examples of community-focused initiatives and activities: The Hammer Museum at the University of California, Los Angeles, serves as a polling place on Election Day (and offers free validated parking to voters). The Worcester Art Museum in Massachusetts hosts naturalization ceremonies for people becoming American citizens. The Montreal Museum of Fine Arts is working with local doctors who can prescribe a museum visit (with free admission) to patients needing to reduce stress. Numerous museums are working both with law enforcement and with medical schools, using close looking at art to help strengthen the observational skills required in those professions.

While building relationships with the people and groups who attend these programs is beneficial for the community, museums have to think about how these relationships can be sustained. The ultimate goal is for people in the community to begin to think of the museum as a resource for them, personally; ideally, they'll be intrigued by their surroundings when they go to vote, say, and the museum can find a way to leverage that intrigue into something more tangible (a visit, a donation, a recommendation to a friend). Closing that loop is key to impacting the museum's sustainability: museums must not just *seem* relevant but must actually *be* relevant.

Looking at the movement on these issues, I think that prospective museum employees are entering the field at a good time. Not all the problems in the field will be solved, and progress might be slow, but as the most diverse generation of Americans in history, young people entering the workforce will bring energy and a commitment to equity that museums have not seen before and will help propel the initiatives outlined here forward. The future museum workplace looks to be one that is more diverse, more equitable, healthier and less stressful for staff, more financially sustainable, and more relevant to the community.

15

Resources

The resources listed here are good starting points for aspiring museum professionals who want to learn more about the field. This is just a small sampling of the available resources; it includes primarily museum- or non-profit-related materials, rather than materials related to the broader context of any particular job. For example, people who want to learn more about marketing in museums should peruse the museum resources and then separately look into books, websites, and publications related to marketing more generally. For the most part the resources I've included are easily readable for non-specialists, and most of the materials can be accessed for free. I also recommend that people who are interested in entering the field go to the websites of museums that intrigue them and sign up for their electronic newsletters; this is a great way to learn about what's going on in one's geographic area and/or area of content interest.

PROFESSIONAL ASSOCIATIONS

Museum professional associations provide extensive resources for their members. Membership rates are quite affordable for students and job seekers; people who are employed at member museums can access resources through the museum's institutional membership. Association conferences offer learning and networking opportunities; conference expenses can often be offset scholarships or by volunteering at the event.

American Alliance of Museums (AAM), aam-us.org
    In addition to general membership, AAM has a variety of Professional Networks (PNs) that focus on most of the major categories of museum professionals' interests

and discipline. The listing of PNs can be found on the AAM website: aam-us.org/
programs/about-aam/professional-networks.

AAM's regional affiliates; each of the six affiliates has an annual conference.
- Association of Midwest Museums (AMM), midwestmuseums.org
- Mid-Atlantic Association of Museums (MAAM), midatlanticmuseums.org
- Mountain Plain Museums Association (MPMA), mpma.net
- New England Museum Association (NEMA), nemanet.org
- Southeastern Museums Conference (SEMC), semcdirect.net
- Western Museums Association (WMA), http://www.westmuse.org

Several states also have museum associations; they are listed on the Coalition of State
Museums Association website, statemuseumassociations.org/directory.

Association of Academic Museums and Galleries, aamg-us.org

American Institute for Conservation of Historic and Artistic Works (AIC),
conservation-us.org
    The professional association for conservators. The AIC website includes detailed
information about training requirements in the conservation field.

Association of Science and Technology Centers (ASTC), astc.org
    The professional association for science museums.

Association of Children's Museums (ACM), childrensmuseums.org
    An international professional organization for children's museums. Hosts an an-
nual conference.

Association of Zoos and Aquariums, www.aza.org
    The professional association and accrediting body for zoos and aquaria. Hosts an
annual conference.

American Association for State and Local History (AASLH), aaslh.org
    The professional association for "history-doers."

Museum Computer Network (MCN), mcn.edu
    An organization whose mission is to "advance digital transformation in muse-
ums." Holds an annual conference.

Museum Educators' Roundtable (MER), museumedu.org
    MER publishes the *Journal of Museum Education* (listed under Publications, fol-
lowing) as well as a blog.

MuseumNext, museumnext.com

A London-based organization that holds international conferences about the future of museums. Many of the talks from past conferences are available for free on the MuseumNext website.

MuseWeb, museweb.net

An organization for professionals in museum technology.

National Association for Interpretation (NAI), interpnet.com

An organization "dedicated to advancing the profession of heritage interpretation." Holds an international conference and regular training and certification courses.

National Emerging Museum Professional Network, nationalempnetwork.org/

An organization that supports all self-defined "emerging" museum professionals. Many cities across the country have local chapters. Has a free newsletter.

BLOGS

AASLH Blog, aaslh.org/blog

Useful articles for history museum professionals.

Alliance Labs, aam-us.org/category/alliance-labs

AAM's blog covers a wide range of topics, written by professionals from across the country.

AAM's *Center for the Future of Museums Blog*, aam-us.org/category/future-of-museums

By Elizabeth Merritt; looks at current trends and indicators of future events and scenarios that may affect museums. Also publishes an excellent weekly newsletter, *Dispatches from the Future of Museums*, and an annual *Trendswatch*.

Art Museum Teaching, artmuseumteaching.com

By Mike Murawski; despite its name, this blog covers topics that affect the museum world at large—not just art museums and not just educators. Many posts focus on community engagement and inclusive practice in museums.

Leadership Matters, leadershipmatters1213.wordpress.com

By Anne Ackerson and Joan Baldwin, this blog explores twenty-first-century museum leadership.

Know Your Own Bone, colleendilen.com

By Colleen Dillenschneider; this blog presents market research and behavioral economics relevant to leaders of cultural organizations.

Joyful Museums, joyfulmuseums.com
   By Marieke Van Damme; this blog explores ways to create positive workplace culture and presents the annual "Museum Worker Engagement Survey."

Museum 2.0, museumtwo.blogspot.com
   Nina Simon focuses on participatory, community-based museums and museum programs.

Nonprofit AF, nonprofitaf.com
   By Vu Le; a thoughtful, funny, and irreverent blog about non-profit work, with a focus on equity and inclusion for non-profit staff (to whom he refers as "unicorns") as well as the people we serve—plus, cute pictures of baby animals!

Incluseum, incluseum.com
   Rose Paquet Kinsley and Alethia Wittman look at issues related to inclusion in museums.

ExhibiTricks, blog.orselli.net
   By Paul Orselli; this blog focuses primarily on museum exhibit design and development, but also looks at other field-wide topics.

PERIODICALS

Online only:

Hyperallergic, hyperallergic.com/about
   Articles about art, culture, exhibitions, galleries, and museums. Also has a daily newsletter.

New England Museums Now, nemanet.org/resources/publications/new-england -museums-now.
   Published twice annually by NEMA; the current issue is always free on the NEMA site.

Print and online:

History News, published by AASLH, aaslh.org/resources/publications
   Access to the journal is restricted to members, but prospective members can download a sample issue from the website.

Journal of Museum Education, museumedu.org/journal/jme-online
   Published by the Museum Education Roundtable. The only peer-reviewed journal about museum education. Though access to the *Journal of Museum Education*

through the Museum Education Roundtable's site requires membership, many college and university libraries (especially those with museum studies programs) have access via their journals database.

Museum Magazine, aam-us.org/programs/museum-magazine
 Published by AAM. While full issues are a member benefit, several articles are always available for free on the AAM website.

The New York Times special Museums Section, nytimes.com/spotlight/museums -special-section
 Published annually, looks at trends in US and international museums.

Nonprofit Quarterly, nonprofitquarterly.org
 A print and online magazine about a wide variety of issues in the non-profit world at large. Has an excellent free newsletter.

The Nonprofit Times, thenonprofittimes.com/about
 Aimed at executives running non-profit organizations. Has a free newsletter and many free resources online.

Technical Leaflets, https://aaslh.org/resources/publications/
 Brief how-to guides on specific topics, published by AASLH. Members receive them in *History News* magazine; hundreds are available for purchase on the AASLH site for a small fee.

BOOKS

Ackerson, Anne W., and Joan H. Baldwin. *Leadership Matters*. New York: AltaMira Press, 2019.
 This landmark book about leadership in museums, which was recently updated, was the genesis of the *Leadership Matters* blog.

Baldwin, Joan H., and Anne W. Ackerson. *Women in the Museum: Lessons from the Workplace*. New York: Routledge, 2017.
 The first book to look comprehensively at women in the museum workplace, from a historical and contemporary perspective, as well as from the point of view of women entering the field. Based on research and extensive first-hand accounts of women working throughout the museum field.

Beaulieu, Rebekah, Dawn E. Salerno, and Mark S. Gold, eds. *The State of Museums: Voices from the Field*. Boston: MuseumsEtc, 2018.
 This book looks at a wide range of issues and topics in museums today. (Full disclosure: I wrote the chapter on museum studies programs.)

Blake, Jenny. *Pivot: The Only Move That Matters Is Your Next One.* New York: Portfolio, 2017.
A useful book for anyone considering a career change from another field into museums.

Genoways, Hugh H., Lynne M. Ireland, and Cinnamon Catlin-Legutko, eds. *Museum Administration 2.0.* New York: Rowman & Littlefield, 2017.
A comprehensive volume about the details of administration in terms of finance, law, ethics, facilities, marketing, collections, and more.

Norris, Linda, and Rainey Tisdale. *Creativity in Museum Practice.* Walnut Creek, CA: Left Coast Press, 2014.
A fun and creative book about leadership, motivation, and teamwork relevant to all levels of museum staff.

Simon, Nina. *The Art of Relevance.* Santa Cruz, CA: Museum 2.0, 2016.
———. *The Participatory Museum.* Santa Cruz, CA: Museum 2.0, 2010.
These two books by the former director of the Museum of Art and History in Santa Cruz, California, look at ways to make museums relevant to their communities. Both are highly readable.

Stevens, Greg, and Wendy Luke, eds. *A Life in Museums: Managing Your Museum Career.* Washington, DC: The AAM Press, 2012.
An excellent overview of a wide spectrum of topics for all stages of a museum career, from résumé writing to mentoring.

PODCASTS

History of the World in 100 Objects, britishmuseum.org/explore/a_history_of_the
_world.aspx
Produced by the British Museum and the BBC in 2010. This podcast is narrated by then-director of the British Museum, Neil MacGregor. A fascinating compendium of stories revealed by objects from across time and around the world. Regardless of one's role in a museum, understanding the power of objects is key.

Museum People, nemanet.org/nema-community/museum-people
Produced by the New England Museum Association (NEMA). Hosted by NEMA Executive Director Dan Yaeger and Marieke Van Damme, NEMA board member and director of the Cambridge Historical Society in Massachusetts. Includes interviews with museum staff people about their paths and what they do in their jobs.

Museopunks, labs.aam-us.org/museopunks/
Produced by the AAM; covers a wide range of topics in museums and showcases museum staff and projects from across the country.

Working, http://www.slate.com/articles/podcasts/working.html
The series, produced by Slate, is wide-ranging, but there have been quite a few episodes featuring museum professionals in different types of jobs.

WHITE PAPERS AND REPORTS

White papers are in-depth reports that outline a topic of interest to the field and explain the presenting organization's position. White papers are published on an as-needed basis, and there is no central clearinghouse for them. Here, I list a few sources, but an online search for the term "museum white paper" leads to many more. Searches by topic will yield results with a broader scope not limited to museums.

AAM; search "white paper" on aam-us.org
Some of AAM's white papers are available to members only, but others are free. Two examples: "Direct Care of Collections: Ethics, Guidelines, and Recommendations" (2016), which defines a term related to the proper use of funds from object deaccessioning, and "Building the Future of Education: Museums and Learning Ecosystem" (2014).

NEMA, nemanet.org/resources/publications/white-papers/
All of NEMA's white papers, which cover a variety of topics, are available for free download.

Bell, Jeanne, and Marla Cornelius. "Underdeveloped: A National Study of Challenges Facing Nonprofit Fundraising." San Francisco: Compass Point and Evelyn and Walter Haas, Jr. Fund, 2013.
An essential read for anyone interested in museum development.

OTHER TOOLS

Guidestar, guidestar.org
A clearinghouse for financial information from non-profits, based on their tax returns. Free registration allows users to download the entire 990 tax form from an organization, which provides crucial information about the museum's income, expenses, and institutional priorities. Form 990s typically include a list of board members and the salary of the highest-paid employees, which can be useful for

benchmarking. Guidestar also has its own useful publications, including a line-by-line guide to understanding 990s, on its "Resources & Content" page.

Massachusetts Institute of Technology's Living Wage Calculator, livingwage.mit.edu/
   This tool allows users to calculate the cost of living in any given community. Such information can be helpful in weighing job opportunities and negotiating salaries.

Pew Research, pewresearch.org
   A "nonpartisan fact tank" that serves as a clearinghouse for all manner of fascinating public opinion and demographic information. Of particular interest is the "Generations and Age" topic as it relates to the workplace, but other data about societal trends is also worthwhile in terms of how those trends might affect museum visitation.

Toastmasters, toastmaster.org
   The website of the communication and leadership development organization where many non-profit professionals hone their public speaking skills. The website includes information about where chapters are located. Membership costs around one hundred dollars per year, depending on location.

Notes

CHAPTER 1: FROM ART TO ZOOLOGY

1. Susie Wilkening, "Older Adult Museum-Goers: A Data Story," Wilkening Consulting, last modified 2017, accessed August 9, 2018, http://www.wilkeningconsulting.com/uploads/8/6/3/2/86329422/wilkening_consulting_data_story_-_older_adults.pdf.

2. "Visit," Brooklyn Children's Museum, accessed August 9, 2018, https://www.brooklynkids.org/visit/.

3. "Accreditation by the Numbers," AAM, accessed August 7, 2018, https://www.aam-us.org/programs/accreditation-excellence-programs/accreditation-by-the-numbers/.

4. Note that AAM's percentages for both staff and budget size represent *accredited* museums. Because micro and small museums are less likely than larger ones to have the capacity (meaning staff time, expertise, or funding) to apply for accreditation, they are undoubtedly underrepresented here, and make up a larger percentage of museums as a whole.

5. "Accreditation by the Numbers," AAM.

6. "Accreditation by the Numbers," AAM.

7. Here, "private" refers to ownership, not to access. Private museums are required to be open to the public to receive non-profit status. The term "non-profit" refers to an institution's tax status under section 501(c)(3) of the Internal Revenue Service's tax code (in fact, you'll often hear non-profits referred to as "501(c)(3)s"). Non-profit status does not mean that the organization cannot be profitable; however, the primary objective of the institution must be to fulfill its mission, and profits must be reinvested toward that goal.

CHAPTER 2: ORGANIZATIONAL STRUCTURE

1. A list of board members is also included on the museum's tax return, which can be viewed for free at guidestar.org.

2. If this sounds intimidating, starting with a small local organization may be the best approach. Board service doesn't have to be in museums to be useful; in fact, volunteering at a non-profit outside of the field may be better for broadening one's understanding of the sector. Social service, health, animal welfare, or educational non-profits are some of the many options.

CHAPTER 3: THE FRONT LINE

1. The terminology within VS can differ significantly from museum to museum. Sometimes VS is used to describe all the front-facing positions, or it can mean just the operation of the front desk. Here, we're using VS more broadly and will use "Admissions" to refer to the ticket sales/front desk. Try not to get caught up in the terminology but instead to focus on the description.

2. Similarly, admissions staff shouldn't make any assumptions about visitors' relationships to each other. A great resource for appropriate language to use when greeting families is the Family Inclusive Language Chart, developed by Margaret Middleton, available for free download at her website, margaretmiddleton.com.

3. At jumbo museums, separate shops may cater to different clientele. For example, museums with large numbers of school groups will often have a separate kiosk featuring very inexpensive items (under five dollars) so that the shop staff can better serve kids, and teachers/chaperones don't have to worry about bringing groups into the larger shop. At the other end of the spectrum, museums might have a high-end gallery. For example, the Heard Museum in Phoenix, Arizona, has both the "Books & More" shop—a typical museum store—and the "Heard Museum Shop," which is a gallery of art and traditional crafts made by Native artists.

4. Depending on the size of the museum, the manager role described here may actually be carried out by multiple people. For example, a jumbo museum might have more than one buyer, and might have one person who focuses on the display of items. In a micro museum, one person will do all of the above plus other VS tasks.

5. In some cases, other museum positions are included in the union along with security guards.

6. While I can't cite evidence to this fact, I know from experience in the field that many security guards in art museums are artists themselves, and find being around the artwork to be one of the best perks of the job.

7. Fortunately, museums may allow security staff to read or sketch if it's slow. Anyone who has visited a museum on a very quiet day might have noticed this!

CHAPTER 4: EDUCATION

1. In the case of kindergarten to twelfth-grade groups, these visits are otherwise known as "field trips," a term that has gone out of favor in museums because it suggests that the visits are an extra and not an essential part of the school curriculum.

2. Confusingly, sometimes "group tour" or "school tour" is used to refer to the entire experience at the museum, even if it includes additional activities.

3. The Denver Art Museum is one prominent example of this model. Each collection area, such as Native Arts and Asian Art, has a "Master Teacher" who is a specialist in that particular content.

4. Though telephone communication has been largely replaced by email communication in many parts of the museum, the coordinator job still relies heavily on the phone.

5. This term can create confusion when used with people who are not versed in museum terminology—their first association might be with a language or sign language interpreter rather than a museum educator.

6. "Docents," from the Latin word *docere*, to teach, are usually volunteers, though not always. In some museums, docent volunteers are the main interpreters, working with all school groups and visitors who request tours. While I greatly value the work and dedication of these volunteers, I am gratified to see many museums redefining the docent role and using more paid interpreters to interact with visitors. This is a skilled role that should be treated as a professional position. If the field relies on unpaid volunteers to carry out this core mission-related function, we are literally devaluing the important work an interpreter does.

7. Psychologist Abraham Maslow's "Hierarchy of Needs" is a theory that is often referenced in museum education. It describes what needs a visitor must have met—in sequential order—to be able to engage in creative activities, like learning at a museum. This Khan Academy video is a good introduction to the theory: https://www.khanacademy.org/test-prep/mcat/behavior/theories-personality/v/maslow-hierarchy-of-needs.

8. First-person interpretation is becoming more rare as it can be harder for visitors to engage with; it's seen as more of a novelty than as an opportunity for meaningful conversation.

9. I would argue that content knowledge is less important than skill at interacting with people: it's easier to learn the content on the job than it is to learn the interpersonal skills.

CHAPTER 5: WORKING WITH OBJECTS

1. Kimberly Bradley, "Why Museums Hide Masterpieces Away," www.bbc.com, last modified January 23, 2015, accessed September 17, 2018, http://www.bbc.com/culture/story/20150123-7-masterpieces-you-cant-see.

2. A couple of recent examples are Francesca Faridany's role in *Black Panther* (though a real curator would not bring her coffee into the galleries!) and Nicole Kidman's role in *Paddington*.

3. Note that an assistant curator and a curatorial assistant are two distinct jobs: the former is a junior curator, whereas the latter is an administrative job and typically not on the curatorial track.

4. "Curatorial Departments," The Metropolitan Museum of Art, accessed September 4, 2018, https://www.metmuseum.org/about-the-met/curatorial-departments.

5. An example of this occurred when the Higgins Armory Museum in Worcester, Massachusetts, ceased operations; the Worcester Art Museum received the key works from the closed museum as part of a merger agreement. The arms and armor collection at Worcester Art Museum is known as the Higgins Collection and has a dedicated curator.

6. Society of American Archivists, "What Are Archives?," https://www2.archivists.org/, accessed September 17, 2018, https://www2.archivists.org/about-archives.

CHAPTER 6: EXHIBITIONS

1. Exhibition equipment is often stored offsite, whereas onsite storage space—which is often at a premium—is reserved for collection objects.
2. While many large and jumbo museums have dedicated audiovisual staff that can install equipment for sound and video, in smaller museums, as Margo Lentz-Meyer explains in this chapter's profile, this task is part of the preparator's job.

CHAPTER 7: CONSERVATION

1. "Core Documents: Commentaries to the Guidelines for Practice: Commentary 22—Materials and Methods," American Institute for Conservation of Historic and Artistic Works, accessed October 1, 2018, http://www.conservation-us.org/our-organizations/association-(aic)/governance/code-of-ethics-and-guidelines-for-practice/commentaries-to-the-guidelines-for-practice-(html)/22#.W7InABNKh-U.
2. "Museum Conservation," The J. Paul Getty Museum, accessed October 1, 2018, http://www.getty.edu/museum/conservation/index.html.

CHAPTER 8: COMMUNICATIONS

1. According to Colleen Dilenschneider, 30 percent of the US market is made up of non-visitors to cultural institutions, and 38 percent of the market can be categorized as "unlikely visitors." Only 32 percent of the US market can be considered "high propensity visitors," or people who either do attend or are likely to attend cultural institutions. "The Key to Reaching New Audiences for Cultural Organizations," colleendilen.com, accessed October 14, 2018, https://www.colleendilen.com/2017/11/15/reach-likely-visitors-not-attending-cultural-organizations-data/.
2. Read the Code of Ethics on the American Alliance for Museums' website: https://www.aam-us.org/programs/ethics-standards-and-professional-practices/code-of-ethics-for-museums/.

CHAPTER 9: DEVELOPMENT

1. Each museum defines a "major" gift differently, depending on the size of the budget and the median of the other donations. A small museum might consider five thousand dollars the minimum for a major gift; a mid-size museum ten thousand dollars; a large or jumbo museum fifty thousand dollars.
2. Jeanne Bell and Marla Cornelius, *Underdeveloped: A National Study of Challenges Facing Nonprofit Fundraising* (San Francisco: Compass Point and Evelyn and Walter Haas, Jr. Fund, 2013), p. 6.
3. "Paying Commission on Grant Proposals: Don't Do It," *The Non Profit Times*, last modified May 13, 2014, accessed October 22, 2018, http://www.thenonprofittimes.com/news-articles/paying-commission-grant-proposals-dont/.

CHAPTER 10: THE EXECUTIVE OFFICE

1. "Ex officio" in Latin, means "from the office." In this case, it means essentially that the director's position, rather than the individual, sits on the committee. If a person left the role, she would relinquish that seat to the new director.

2. As the governing body, the board officially delegates authority for the day-to-day management to the director.

3. A current strategic plan is one of the five "Core Documents" currently required for accreditation by the American Alliance of Museums.

4. "Office of Presidential Libraries," www.archives.gov, accessed October 27, 2018, https://www.archives.gov/presidential-libraries/about/office.html.

CHAPTER 11: ADMINISTRATION

1. Learn more about GAAP at www.accountingfoundation.org.

CHAPTER 12: UNIVERSAL SKILLS AND DISTINCT PATHWAYS

1. Stephen Covey, "Habit 3: Put First Things First," www.franklincovey.com, accessed October 31, 2018, https://www.franklincovey.com/the-7-habits/habit-3.html.

2. For further discussion of museum studies programs, see my chapter "The Value of Museum Studies" in *The State of Museums: Voices from the Field*. Boston: MuseumsEtc, 2018.

CHAPTER 13: THINGS I WISH I HAD KNOWN WHEN I WAS TWENTY-FOUR

1. The estimation of what is acceptable and unacceptable in a work situation will change over time as one's life circumstances do. It's worth revisiting this equation every five years or so.

CHAPTER 14: WHERE ARE MUSEUMS GOING?

1. John Boitnott, "How the Baby Boomers' Exit Will Affect the Way You Do Business," *Inc.*, February 9, 2016, https://www.inc.com/john-boitnott/how-to-bridge-the-talent-gap-as-baby-boomers-leave-your-company.html.

2. Roger Schonfeld, Mariët Westermann, and Liam Sweeney, *Art Museum Staff Demographic Survey*, p. 3, July 25, 2015, https://mellon.org/media/filer_public/ba/99/ba99e53a-48d5-4038-80e1-66f9ba1c020e/awmf_museum_diversity_report_aamd_7-28-15.pdf.

3. *American Alliance of Museums Annual Report 2016-2020*, p. 2, February 24, 2016, https://www.aam-us.org/wp-content/uploads/2017/11/english-strat-plan.pdf.

4. Joan Baldwin, "Museum Salary Equity: If You're a Woman, What Does It Mean?," *Leadership Matters* (blog), entry posted September 26, 2016, accessed December 3, 2018, https://leadershipmatters1213.wordpress.com/.

5. Note the broad use of the word "programming" here to mean all mission-critical initiatives, including exhibitions, educational programs, etc.

6. Dawn E. Salerno and Mark S. Gold, "Investing in Museums: A New Paradigm for Professional Compensation." In *The State of Museums: Voices from the Field*, edited by Rebekah Beaulieu, Dawn E. Salerno, and Mark S. Gold, 144–67. Boston: MuseumsEtc., 2018.

7. Sarah Erdman et al., "Leaving the Museum Field," *Alliance Labs* (blog), entry posted September 27, 2017, accessed December 3, 2018, https://www.aam-us.org/2017/09/22/leaving-the-museum-field/.

Bibliography

"Accreditation by the Numbers." American Alliance of Museums. Accessed August 7, 2018. https://www.aam-us.org/programs/accreditation-excellence-programs/accreditation-by -the-numbers/.

American Alliance of Museums Annual Report 2016-2020. February 24, 2016. https://www .aam-us.org/wp-content/uploads/2017/11/english strat-plan.pdf.

Baldwin, Joan. "Museum Salary Equity: If You're a Woman, What Does It Mean?" *Leadership Matters* (blog). Entry posted September 26, 2016. Accessed December 3, 2018. https:// leadershipmatters1213.wordpress.com/.

Bell, Jeanne, and Marla Cornelius. "Underdeveloped: A National Study of Challenges Facing Nonprofit Fundraising." San Francisco: Compass Point and Evelyn and Walter Haas, Jr. Fund, 2013.

Boitnott, John. "How the Baby Boomers' Exit Will Affect the Way You Do Business." *Inc.*, February 9, 2016. https://www.inc.com/john-boitnott/how-to-bridge-the-talent-gap-as -baby-boomers-leave-your-company.html.

Bradley, Kimberly. "Why Museums Hide Masterpieces Away." www.bbc.com. Last modi-fied January 23, 2015. Accessed September 17, 2018. http://www.bbc.com/culture/ story/20150123-7-masterpieces-you-cant-see.

"Core Documents: Commentaries to the Guidelines for Practice: Commentary 22— Materials and Methods." American Institute for Conservation of Historic and Artistic Works. Accessed October 1, 2018. http://www.conservation-us.org/our-organizations/ association-(aic)/governance/code-of-ethics-and-guidelines-for-practice/commentaries-to -the-guidelines-for-practice-(html)/22#.W7InABNKh-U.

Covey, Stephen. "Habit 3: Put First Things First." www.franklincovey.com. Accessed October 31, 2018. https://www.franklincovey.com/the-7-habits/habit-3.html.

"Curatorial Departments." The Metropolitan Museum of Art. Accessed September 4, 2018. https://www.metmuseum.org/about-the-met/curatorial-departments.

Erdman, Sarah, Claudia Ocello, Dawn E. Salerno, and Marieke VanDamme. "Leaving the Museum Field." *Alliance Labs* (blog). Entry posted September 27, 2017. Accessed December 3, 2018. https://www.aam-us.org/2017/09/22/leaving-the-museum-field/.

"The Key to Reaching New Audiences for Cultural Organizations." colleendilen.com. Accessed October 14, 2018. https://www.colleendilen.com/2017/11/15/reach-likely-visitors-not-attending-cultural-organizations-data/.

"Maslow's Hierarchy of Needs." www.khanacademy.org. Accessed September 3, 2018. https://www.khanacademy.org/test-prep/mcat/behavior/theories-personality/v/maslow-hierarchy-of-needs.

"Museum Conservation." The J. Paul Getty Museum. Accessed October 1, 2018. http://www.getty.edu/museum/conservation/index.html.

Norris, Linda, and Rainey Tisdale. *Creativity in Museum Practice*. Walnut Creek, CA: Left Coast Press, 2014.

"Office of Presidential Libraries." www.archives.gov. Accessed October 27, 2018. https://www.archives.gov/presidential-libraries/about/office.html.

"Paying Commission on Grant Proposals: Don't Do It." *The Non Profit Times*. Last modified May 13, 2014. Accessed October 22, 2018. http://www.thenonprofittimes.com/news-articles/paying-commission-grant-proposals-dont/.

Salerno, Dawn E., and Mark S. Gold. "Investing in Museums: A New Paradigm for Professional Compensation." In *The State of Museums: Voices from the Field*, edited by Rebekah Beaulieu, Dawn E. Salerno, and Mark S. Gold, 144–67. Boston: MuseumsEtc., 2018.

Schonfeld, Roger, Mariët Westermann, and Liam Sweeney. *Art Museum Staff Demographic Survey*. July 25, 2015. https://mellon.org/media/filer_public/ba/99/ba99e53a-48d5-4038-80e1-66f9ba1c020e/awmf_museum_diversity_report_aamd_7-28-15.pdf.

Simon, Nina. *The Participatory Museum*. Santa Cruz, CA: Museum 2.0, 2010.

Society of American Archivists. "What Are Archives?" https://www2.archivists.org/. Accessed September 17, 2018. https://www2.archivists.org/about-archives.

"Visit." Brooklyn Children's Museum. Accessed August 9, 2018. https://www.brooklynkids.org/visit/.

Wilkening, Susie. "Older Adult Museum-Goers: A Data Story." Wilkening Consulting. Last modified 2017. Accessed August 9, 2018. http://www.wilkeningconsulting.com/uploads/8/6/3/2/86329422/wilkening_consulting_data_story_-_older_adults.pdf.

Young, Tara. "The Value of Museum Studies." In *The State of Museums: Voices from the Field*, 214–25. Boston: MuseumsEtc, 2018.

Index

Page references for figures are italicized.

About the Author

Tara Young is an independent museum professional who has worked in the field for more than twenty years. Previously, she served as Deputy Director at the Museum of Russian Icons in Clinton, Massachusetts; Director of Education at the Higgins Armory Museum in Worcester, Massachusetts; Associate Curator of Education at the Tacoma Art Museum in Tacoma, Washington; and Assistant Curator of Modern and Contemporary Art at the Seattle Art Museum, where she received the Patterson Simms Curatorial Fellowship. Tara holds a BA from Harvard College and an MA from the University of Pittsburgh, both in History of Art and Architecture. She also has a certificate in Nonprofit Leadership and Management from the Institute for Nonprofit Practice at Tisch College of Civic Life at Tufts University. Tara teaches museum studies at Tufts University, where she was a 2018 Fellow at the Center for the Enhancement of Teaching and Learning. She serves as a peer accreditation reviewer for the American Alliance of Museums. Tara lives in central Massachusetts.